Hands All Around

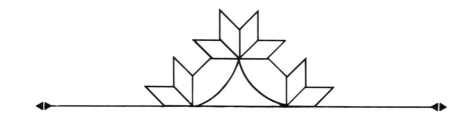

H·A·N·D·S A·L·L
A·R·O·U·N·D
Making Cooperative Quilts

JUDY ROBBINS

GRETCHEN THOMAS

Illustrated by Judy Robbins

VNR VAN NOSTRAND REINHOLD COMPANY

Printed in the United States of America
Designed by Ann Gold

Published by Van Nostrand Reinhold Company Inc.
135 West 50th Street
New York, New York 10020

Van Nostrand Reinhold Company Limited
Molly Millars Lane
Wokingham, Berkshire RG11 2PY, England

Van Nostrand Reinhold
480 La Trobe Street
Melbourne, Victoria 3000, Australia

Macmillan of Canada
Division of Gage Publishing Limited
164 Commander Boulevard
Agincourt, Ontario M1S 3C7, Canada

16 15 14 13 12 11 10 9 8 7 6 5 4 3 2 1

Library of Congress Cataloging in Publication Data
Robbins, Judy.
Hands all around.
Includes index.
1. Quilting.   I. Thomas, Gretchen.   II. Title.
TT835.R6   1984   746.9′7   84-3561
ISBN 0-442-27635-4

DEDICATION

Talk about "hands all around"!
Last Thursday when we were sewing the border strips on our quilt,
it took six hands to maneuver the quilt through the machine,
and I smiled to myself as I remembered the title of your book.
—Millie Dunkel, Carbondale, Illinois

This book is dedicated to the quilters who shared
their craft, their quilts, and their lives with us, and to
the many others who have yet to discover the joys and
satisfactions of making cooperative quilts.

CONTENTS

ACKNOWLEDGMENTS

We are especially indebted to our colleague, Odette Teel, for her generosity to us and her delightful good humor.

Judy: For as long as I can remember, there have been sewing women in my family. I'd particularly like to acknowledge my mother, Doris Hartell, and her mother, Sara Collins, and her mother, Martha Lowe, who all passed along to me the quiet satisfactions of needlework. I have been fortunate to have had many supporters: quilting colleagues and good friends Mickey Lawler, Sheila Meyer, Vikki Chenette, and Sarah Gobes; my father, Andy Hartell, and my sons, Jeffrey, Neil, and Timothy Robbins; my mother-in-law, Anne Robbins; and my dearest friend and companion on the trail, Bruce Robbins. During these intense months of writing, Gretchen Thomas became a good friend as we coparented this book child, stretching ourselves to envision the best for it and laughing together as it asserted itself and went its own headstrong way.

Gretchen: As I worked on *Hands All Around,* I often pictured the following people sitting in chairs near my desk, encouraging, inspiring, and listening to what we had to say: Ruth Groves Thomas and Pearl Lyens Groves, who taught me the art and comforts of needlework; Kathleen Devaney, Ruth Graf, and Bena Kallick, who taught me the craft and satisfactions of writing and advising. Elisabeth Room, Peter Martin, and Lorraine Keeney shared with me the joys of working cooperatively with friends. From Wiley Thomas I learned the importance of seeing in new ways, of questioning everything, and of not stopping until the job was done. When I first saw Judy's sewing machine set up on her desk and her typewriter in use on the ironing board nearby, I knew we'd work wonderfully together, and we have.

Introduction

Hands All Around is a complete handbook of cooperative quiltmaking. By "cooperative quilt," we mean one quilt that is sewn and perhaps designed by more than one person. Sometimes this is also called "group quilt," and we will use the terms interchangeably. Hands All Around is also the name of the beautiful old quilt pattern that embellishes our leading pages. We chose it for our title because it reminds us of the cooperative spirit traditionally associated with quilting in this country.

The old-time quilting bees were an exciting event in an otherwise mundane and often drab routine. They provided a time for women to connect with other women, to pass along news and gossip, and to share joys and problems with empathetic listeners. In the years since the United States Bicentennial in 1976, after a long dormant period, quilting bees have begun to recur with increasing frequency. It is true that our modern ways of living are vastly different from those of our foremothers. We are part of an eventful, uncertain, sometimes chaotic society. One might ask, "How does the modern woman have time to make a group quilt?" Group quilting is not just another activity to add to our already overloaded schedules. Today's cooperative quilter enjoys all the pleasures of the old bees, but she also finds a quiet respite from her hectic daily schedule in the unhurried work of quilting. Noncompetitive, equally shared work is a rare commodity in our society, and women have eagerly rediscovered it at the quilting frame.

Perhaps you have wanted to learn quilting but wondered how you would ever find the time to finish a large quilt. Hands All Around will introduce you to others like yourself who have found that quilting with a group has solved their concerns about time. Detailed here are several plans for time sharing so that you can create quilts quickly while learning a great deal. Perhaps you are a quilter who has never worked with a group. Or perhaps you already belong to a community organization, and you think the whole group might enjoy a learning-by-doing project. The friendly advice and pointers presented here will show you how to get started and organize the work. All kinds of women's clubs, schools, and civic, social, and church groups have used quilts successfully as fundraisers, gifts, commemoratives, and friendship builders. We have collected stories and tips from women all over America who have made an incredibly varied array of quilts. Bicentennial commemoratives, retirement and wedding quilts, birth and birthday quilts, anniversary presents, friendship and thank-you quilts, city, county, town, and state quilts are all commonly made by groups who may or may not have quilted before. One of the quilts we describe commemorates a sled-dog race across Alaska; another celebrates the tropical beauty of Sanibel Island, Florida. The wide variety of projects described here is sure to present a number of possibilities for making quilts that will adapt themselves to your own unique situations.

We offer guidance here, in *Hands All Around,* for gathering a group and making the initial meeting a success, and present proven methods for democratically choosing, designing, and making group quilts. We suggest experimenting with "fabric graphs" and "color palettes"—helpful exercises that enable each of us to become quilt designers. Do you have far-away family and friends? Learn how to make successful "by mail" quilts long distance. Here you'll also find help in devising a custom construction system to fit the manner and circumstance of a group and to increase efficiency.

Quilts make such excellent fund raisers that we include a special supplement to help you sell your quilt profitably. Raffles are but one of many successful ways in which quilts can earn money. Look through these pages for direction that will reduce frustration, false starts, and needless expense.

Behind the guidebook that is *Hands All Around* are the quilters who greatly enriched our initial vision for the book. When we requested information about cooperative quilts, the stacks of letters we received told thoughtful, touching stories about quilts made all over America. Again and again, people wrote candidly about their enthusiasm, commitment, exhilaration, and love. They told stories about their quilts, about their lives, and about the others in their groups. Whenever possible we have tried to allow the spirit, warmth, and humor of these quiltmakers to permeate the book.

The letters and photographs we received triggered hours of discussion as we pondered why the craft of quiltmaking (and group quilting in particular) touches so many elemental themes in women's lives. One theme ran through almost all the letters we received—that group quilts are made with love, and that the combined love of many people working together has a great impact on both the makers and receivers. It is love that enables individuals to move out of their smaller, sometimes petty perspectives and habitual ways of living, and to become, for a while at least, their best selves. Often, quilting bees begin on a note of complaint about the weather, or family members, or job pressures, or health. Then, quickly the negative remarks and feelings fade as people begin the disciplined, rhythmic, comforting practice of quilting. Cooperative quilting brings together the full range of womankind—wealthy and poor, expert and novice, young and old, sophisticated and naïve—on the common ground of shared goals, as we create special quilts with the simple, humble craft of the needle.

C·H·A·P·T·E·R 1

A Sampler of Cooperative Quilts

<big>H</big>ere are some of the stories quiltmakers have shared with us about their quilts, the groups that made them, and the lives sewn into them, stitch by stitch.

Special-Occasion Quilts

Is someone in your family or a close friend getting married, expecting a baby, changing jobs, retiring, moving into a new home, or celebrating an important anniversary? You might want to join with other friends and relatives to mark this happy occasion by making a quilt together. The quilt itself provides a wonderful way to express your love, your support, and your hope that the changes in their lives will bring them joy. If, on the other hand, someone very close to you is leaving your community or if a beloved family member has died, you may find that working on a quilt with others who share your loss will enable you to sort out your own feelings and confront the anxiety that change inevitably brings. Many quilters have found that group quiltmaking has been an aid to healing in times of grief, and that it can be counted on to carry them through a particularly stressful time.

Wedding and anniversary quilts generate feelings of warmth and excitement and bind together the couple's friends and relatives. In fact, almost everyone who told us about making a group wedding quilt said, "And now we're at work on one for her younger brother," or, "This quilt was followed a year later by a crib quilt." Quilts designed for "the happy couple" are often highly personal and unique—like the one Ed Larson designed and six friends made for Barbara and Fred Hecht of Evanston, Illinois. (See C-1 in color section.)

Barbara herself does not own a needle, but she had seen us work on other group quilts and had hinted that she and Fred would love to receive one. Their friend Ed Larson was enthusiastic about designing a wall quilt, keeping their blue living room in mind. Within a week he delivered a full-size drawing and a smaller color sketch. Together we chose fabrics from our collections and divided up the work.

Barbara is an interior decorator. The paint-brush in her hand and her overalls are her usual attire. Fred is a photographer, hence the camera on his shoulder. Barbara's six-year-old, Gabriel, is shown in the bathtub, and both dogs and cats are there. Barbara had just done the bathroom in Laura Ashley wallpaper and tiles, so for that room we used a scrap of Laura Ashley fabric that I had cut off one of Barbara's dresses when I hemmed it for her. And we embroidered a fish picture on the kitchen wall—just like the real one. It was such a group effort that I'm not sure any more who did which part.

Mary Jo Deysach, Evanston, Illinois

Another Illinois wedding quilt (see C-2 in color section) involved many more people, but was made with the same loving spirit and took approximately the same amount of time.

It took us just six months to create an heirloom. When our assistant pastor, Dave Hedlin, announced that he and Carol would be married, the women of our church decided to give them a quilt to show our love. My good friend Joan asked if I would be in charge, and of course I agreed, although the idea sounded rather like being committed for life. I decided to surround the young couple with flowers, and found beautiful drawings by Winifred Walker of plants from the Bible.

To our shock we ran short of kits. Everyone wanted to contribute! We solved that by urging people to pair up on some of the blocks and by signing up others for the quilting. When the squares were handed in we had another shock. They were gorgeous! In some, the stitching was so unique that I was in awe. And all the time, this was kept a secret from Dave and Carol. The week he was on vacation we quilted every day, every hour of the day, in a large room at the church. Many times there was no room at the frame. The extra people would thread needles, wax thread, make coffee, or just sit and enjoy. They got a taste of quilting bee fever and kept coming back.

Jackie Dodson, La Grange Park, Illinois

Wedding and anniversary quilts coordinated by mail are a lovely way to include far-away friends and relatives in the festivities:

We commemorated my parents' fiftieth wedding anniversary with a quilt made from six-inch squares of fabric mailed out in the invitations to friends, neighbors, and relatives. The squares came back embroidered, appliquéd, painted, needlepointed, crocheted—you name it! It was extremely gratifying to sew together the results.

Margaret Cusack, Brooklyn, New York

Everyone seems to love working on something for a baby, and a baby quilt is ideal because it delights the parents as well as the child. Nine months gives plenty of lead time for making a crib-sized quilt. One drawback, however, is that most baby quilts are too small to place in a quilting frame, and passing the quilt from person to person for quilting deprives the makers of the fellowship of a quilting bee. The Quilters Guild of Greater Kansas City inadvertently overcame this problem when they chose a Missouri Puzzle pattern for a crib quilt for Samuel Reid Bond, the son of their governor, Christopher Bond. It took a great deal of meeting together for fellowship and mutual support just to piece and block the 3,000 pieces, some of which were only two-thirds of an inch square!

Another consideration is whether to make a wallhanging for the baby's sleeping area or a quilt to be used as bedding—one that may be pressed into service as a fort roof, boat deck, or flying carpet if it survives its early years as "the" blanket.

After having made several traditional baby quilts, a group may tire of the patterns that are customarily used for babies. Remember, there is nothing that prevents baby quilts from exhibiting a wider range of colors, themes, and designs. The wall quilt made for Ann and Peter Diamantini's baby, Joseph, is a good example (figure 1).

Quilts mark transitions, as well as beginnings. We've learned about quilt guild officers, classroom teachers, daycare providers, secretaries, priests, school principals, college administrators, librarians, and extension agents who were all presented with retirement quilts to honor their years of service. These quilts were made by colleagues who, more often than not, were newcomers to needlework. The fun of keeping the secret and the desire to honor the retiree's hard work and commitment carried these novices through the discouragements of lumpy batting, mismatched points, and bleeding fingers.

I was secretary for our town's Newcomers Club, and my best friend was president. Since she had dragged me to my first quilting lessons, I decided we should make her a friendship quilt when she left office. It was kept a secret the whole time, and in a very small town (one square mile) with a club of over one hundred, that is rather amazing! At least eighty women worked on it, and we ended up making two quilts. The energy and enthusiasm it generated were just wonderful.

Anne Bedser, Jenkintown, Pennsylvania.

1. Green Acres Bird Quilt.

These retirement quilts could as easily be called friendship or gratitude quilts, because in addition to marking a life passage they express the deeply felt gratitude of friends who have worked together daily, often for many years.

Hope Martin had been an extension agent for 25 years. As newly elected president of the St. Mary's Extension Homemakers Council, I knew choosing a retirement gift would be one of my first concerns. It had to be something that would not sit on a shelf and collect dust, or be tucked away in a box. One April evening the idea came to me: a quilt with the members' names embroidered on it! But I didn't know how to quilt, and the few members who did were unable to undertake such a large project.

The newly formed Ark and Dove Quilters and their instructor, Ora Norris, also knew Hope, who had been instrumental in forming the quilting guild. Ora offered to do the final quilting, provided she had ample time. Council members Louise Dean and her mother, Grace Loffler, agreed with Ora that the piecing should be done by hand. They felt so strongly about it that they volunteered to do the piecing themselves! Jean Frost was in charge of getting the squares from Louise to the different members to embroider their signatures. The squares were passed back and forth at different meetings, often in Hope's presence, but she never had the slightest idea what we were up to.

There were 250 members and friends present when we gave Hope her quilt a year later. Nothing we could have given would have pleased her more.

Roberta Kieliger, Charlotte Hall, Maryland

House Quilts, Historic Quilts, and Quilts That Tell Life Stories

People have feelings of pride, attachment, and love for their homes and community as deep as those for their family and friends. We often treat our houses as extensions of ourselves, devoting to them the best of our energies, as well as our long-term skills and creativity. It is not surprising, therefore, that houses are a universal theme, chosen by many groups as the subject of cooperative quilts. Members of the Dayton (Washington) Historical Depot Society joined with expert needleworkers to make and raffle a quilt of Dayton's historic homes and buildings (figure 2):

We wanted to preserve the history of these houses and buildings as well as to raise money for the depot restoration. Dayton is well known for its high percentage of homes built before Washington became a state in 1889. We pored over old deeds and maps and then conducted interviews to learn the history of each building. Our findings were all compiled into a booklet presented to the raffle winner. One of the exciting—though unexpected—results was an increased interest in restoring houses all around town.

Darlene Broughton and Faye Rainwater, Dayton, Washington

A similar quilt that contains many historic houses was made by the Ferndale (California) Quilters of their own homes (see C-3 in color section). Quilting teacher Mary Ann Spencer suggested using the traditional House on a Hill pattern for the basic structure of the house blocks, but then encouraged each needleworker to add details—animals, children, fences, house trim, and landscape—to identify the house as her own.

Then there are the twelve members of the Ladies of the Evening Quilt Club, who made a quilt depicting a single house:

The basic design for the Lote House Quilt [see C-4 in color section] came from the fertile imagination of Cynthia Biagiotti. Because we all recognized the problem of scale and proportion, it seemed advisable to have a careful layout. What could be worse than a house built by committee? In addition, we were all determined to make the quilt so that it could be used as either a wallhanging or a bedcover—the quilt would fit on a single bed, with the sky covering the pillow and the picket fence hanging over the side.

Aloyse Yorko, Tequesta, Florida

2. Dayton Historical Houses.

Two intriguing house quilts—one made by the Five Easy Piecers of Berkeley, California, and the other by the Weston, Massachusetts Quilt Workshop—caught our attention:

When my turn came around in our Five Easy Piecers quilt group, I asked my friends to help me make one based on the New England–style houses pictured in the Americana Calendar by Charles Wysocki [see C-5 in color section]. Each of us machine-pieced a building. I provided a few shades of blue and green for the sky and grass and asked them to coordinate their colors with these. I pieced sets of trees to even up the blocks, added the borders, and planned the quilting. The six of us quilted it for two months, and I finished it up.

Mabry Benson, Kensington, California

The Weston quilt was inspired by well-known quiltmaker Jinny Beyer's intricate medallion quilts, with their rich colors and patterned borders. Since Jinny had developed a line of fabrics for a large manufacturer, this made her distinctive "Beyer

look" available to everyone. Mary Lou Smith bought several yards of these fabrics to share with the nine members of the Weston Quilt Workshop. Each person would make a 12-inch block of a house from pieces of Jinny Beyer fabric, supplemented with fabrics of her own. To set the nine houses together, Nancy Halpern hit upon connecting them by streets, complete with road dividers and chromium yellow highway signs. These houses were not to be confused with the ordinary tract development, however, and Rhoda Cohen made sure of this by adding a zingy chevron-print border with deliberately nonmatching corners. The group good-naturedly dubbed their very unusual quilt Beyer Beware. (See C-6 in color section.)

Many quilters had their first group-quilting experience during the 1976 Bicentennial celebration. Gladys Boalt designed the Putnam County (New York) Quilt (see C-7 in color section) to tell the history of the area in scenes that read chronologically across the quilt. In contrast, the Boone (Boone County, Indiana) Bicentennial Sampler (figure 3) was made in 12 sections, each coordinated by its own township committee. Treva Iddings orchestrated the work, her main purpose being to involve as many people as possible. By the time it was hung, over 2,500 people had participated in its making! The women who planned the Oberlin (Ohio) Quilt in 1974 (figure 4) thought it would take them two years to complete it in time for the Bicentennial. They enjoyed working together so much that the quilt was finished in five months. Another group in Carbondale, Illinois, actually took the completed blocks for the 1982 Carbondale Historical Quilt and locked them up in a bank vault until they were ready to be joined together—that's how precious they were.

The women who drew, appliquéd, and embroidered these quilts inevitably became interested in the history they were illustrating. No doubt this has been true for quilters throughout the years, but today's women have learned to do what their grandmothers failed to do: document their work. Many have kept journals that record both the making of their quilts and the histories those quilts portray. Very readable accounts have grown out of needleworker/historian partnerships. Every "historical quilter" shares this hope of Olive Rhines, one of the Hancock (New Hampshire) Quiltmakers (figure 5):

If there is still a town of Hancock, New Hampshire, and a historical society to celebrate the

3 (above). Boone Bicentennial Sampler.

5 (left). Quilting the Hancock Quilt.

Tricentennial in 2079, this quilt should be a tangible, colorful reminder of the pleasurable and worthwhile efforts of the ladies of 1979.

This country's Bicentennial brought quiltmaking into the arena of local historical societies—and the making of historical quilts into the programs of local quilt guilds—and today the practice continues.

Natural outgrowths of the 1976 efforts have been quilts depicting historic houses, quilts about a particular neighborhood or city and quilts that give the history of a particular organization, family, or person.

Quiltmaker Joyce Whittier in Olathe, Kansas, believes that every community should have its own quilt:

A quilt enables residents to express pride in their area's history, accomplishments, and unique features. But before you decide to make a quilt for a city, town, or historical society, make sure they *want* a quilt and are able to display, clean, and store it properly. Work with city officials and art-

4. Oberlin Quilt.

6 (right). Scenes of San Francisco.

7 (above). Scenes of San Francisco;
Golden Gate Bridge block.

ists on the theme and design. Our work with the art commission helped upgrade quilting in our community from "only a craft" to a recognized art.

A "city quilt" was created for the culture and heritage category of a Baltimore quilt contest. The Summer Hill Quilters group had formed just before the announcement of Baltimore's Best Quilting Contest, and the idea of making a contest quilt as their first group effort was a bit intimidating. Nevertheless, the exciting design (see C-9 in color section) generated much enthusiasm, and the more experienced quilters taught the others many techniques during the next nine months. Because the winning quilts would become the property of the city, the group was asked to copyright the design. It portrays important places and facets of culture representing many aspects of life in Baltimore, all projecting out from the center of the city. Historic buildings are quilted with dark thread on the colorful rays, and the city seal is on the reverse side.

Working together to make this prize-winning quilt taught us more about quilting than many of us would have learned on our own with years of effort, and our understanding and caring about each other has grown greatly from our hours around the quilt frame.

Phyllis Wilkinson, Phoenix, Maryland

Another city quilt came from Washington, D.C.:

Washington Perspective 1982 [see C-10 in color section] started as an advanced quilting class project and grew to have a life of its own. We wanted to make an exhibition quilt that would reflect the many reasons why we love Washington, D.C., which is for most of us an adopted city. We took a year and a half to complete it, meeting on Monday mornings. My conclusion is that a successful group project takes time—at least a year—if the kind of experience that produced the Capitol Quilters is to evolve: the experience of learners becoming their own teachers, of students becoming close friends, and of a project involving a thousand decisions becoming a prize-winning reality. As a group, these students learned to set aside individual differences, sought to understand and accept each other's goals, and discovered solutions to each other's problems. They cared about one another, and they forged lasting bonds of friendship.

Mary Coyne Penders, Vienna, Virginia

A unique type of contemporary historic quilt has evolved, which focuses on scenes and symbols of personal importance in the present-day lives of its creators. The Cambridge Women's Quilt (see C-11 in color section) is a fully developed example. Each block depicts a woman or girl actively working or playing in a scene from her own life or the life of someone important to her. This quilt grew out of an oral history project sponsored by the Cambridge Arts Council, and is part of a series of projects that honors individual women's lives and provides situations in which women of different ages and backgrounds can work together and learn about each other. Thus the work on the quilt included collecting oral histories of everyone involved in the project.

The idea that women's lives are important is a very profound one, which challenges many people's definitions of history and their ideas about women's roles.

We knew that if our quilt was to actually include images and stories from women representing the various cultural communities in Cambridge, we would have to make the project accessible to people who don't usually volunteer for activities like this. . . . People being segregated from one another because of age is as strong a source of

isolation as any that exists in this society, creating a great loss in our lives. Older people have acquired a lot of wisdom, and important strategies for coping and surviving. Their stories can greatly enrich the lives of younger people. And younger people bring a sense of vitality and inquisitiveness to an intergenerational project that can energize the older people with whom they are working. . . . But for people of different ages and backgrounds to really collaborate requires that they acknowledge and respect their different values and lifestyles. It has been very exciting to watch women and girls from extremely diverse backgrounds come to understand that they share many common experiences and concerns: concern for the quality of life in their homes and communities, and constraints on their abilities to make choices about the directions of their lives, for instance. The quilting project was designed to help women and girls think about these issues by providing them with a context in which they could express their own stories and then compare them.

Cindy Cohen, Cambridge, Massachusetts

An exciting and unique quiltmaking effort occurred during the 1983 Iditarod Sled-Dog Race. This two-and-a-half-week race takes mushers and dogs over 1,000 miles through checkpoints from Anchorage to Nome, Alaska. It seems fitting that a quilt made to document and benefit a race should itself have become a race to the finish.

A friend and artist who has run the race twice provided drawings of each of the 26 checkpoints. We farmed out squares to anyone who would take them. This proved to have a few drawbacks, but we had no real disasters. As we were continuing merrily onward, we learned there were actually 28 checkpoints this year. Since our layout called for 26 checkpoints and four special corners, we had to make some quick changes. Just when we'd settled on a solution—by this time the front-runners were well on their way to Nome—it was announced that one of the checkpoints had been destroyed by bears and would not be used. What to do with only 27 checkpoints? We left that square in, but made it a large reverse-appliqué paw print. For the two "extra" squares we chose first a map of Alaska showing the trail route with the names of the previous winners, and then for the last, the name of this year's winner and his official time. In the borders are the names of every musher (69 of them) who left Anchorage. Mushers who scratched along the way have a thin red line embroidered through their names.

Our plan was to have the quilt ready to be auctioned at the mushers' banquet, usually held the third evening after the first musher arrives in Nome. Weather for the race was ideal, and the mushers moved along at almost record pace. We prayed for blizzards, but none materialized! We realized we couldn't possibly finish, but someone on the Iditarod Trail Committee suggested that we complete the top and auction it with the notation that it would be finished "to order." What a terrific idea! We actually com-

pleted the top about half an hour before the banquet began.

The response was great and, as anticipated, the mushers were the ones who really loved it. It would have raised even more money for the trail committee if we'd finished it in time to display it. We had fun, we learned, we made some new friends, and we contributed in our own way to "The Last Great Race." Afterwards, we were asked if we planned to make a quilt for the next year's race. Our immediate response was a resounding *no!*, but we soon found ourselves discussing what another quilt might look like and what we'd do differently.

Stephanie Barnett, Nome, Alaska

Fundraising Quilts

Quilts like the Iditarod Race Quilt have been raffled, auctioned, or sold for many purposes by many kinds of groups. The list of groups and causes below was compiled from correspondence with many quilting groups. We hope it will inspire new possibilities for your own fundraising efforts.

The themes and designs of these quilts also range far and wide. Here, for example, are the names of quilts made by two California PTA groups over the last seven years: Alphabet Quilt, Calendar Quilt, Whales and Their Friends, Pond Life, In the Redwoods, Carnival, Toy Store, Our Town, Once

Upon a Time, Children's Stories (figure 8), Rainbow Fantasy (figure 9), Flying Machines—Up, Up, and Away (figure 10), and Creatures under Water, on the Land, and in the Sky.

One traditional way to raise funds through quiltmaking is to incorporate signatures into a quilt, increasing its earning potential by charging individuals to have their name embroidered on it or by soliciting celebrities' signatures. The finished quilt may be raffled or sold. The group that Jan Martin of Caledonia, Ohio, was part of decided to make a signature quilt to raise money for the celebration of

These groups have gathered to make fundraising quilts:

friends	high-school band boosters
quilt guilds	American Field Service
local quilting groups	supporters
churches	4-H clubs
senior citizen centers	Scout troops
teachers' centers	hospital guilds
mother-child centers	historical societies
community centers	herb societies
women's clubs	volunteer firefighters'
newcomers' clubs	supporters
faculty women's clubs	League of Women Voters
alumni associations	chapters
library associations	animal care and study
sports team supporters	centers
parent-teacher	museum volunteers
associations	

These are some of the causes for which funds have been raised:

replenishing a group's	purchasing school
treasury	computers
contributing to	sending a sports team to
church funds	England
covering quilt show	celebrating historic
expenses	occasions
supporting medical	restoring old buildings
research	building new buildings
supporting a political	promoting a museum
campaign	store
providing scholarships	planting trees
building children's	protecting birds and
playgrounds	marine mammals and
	their habitats

8 (above, left). Children's Stories.

9 (above, right). Rainbow Fantasy.

10 (left). Flying Machines—Up, Up, and Away.

the centennial of their church and the bicentennial of the Methodist movement in America, both of which occurred in the same year. Church members paid $3.00 each to have their names embroidered on the simple Nine Patch Quilt. By the time it was completed, the 360 pieces were filled with names of members, founders, and former pastors. In Colchester, Connecticut, Peter Martin tells of making a banner to hang in the teachers' center. Supporters of the center—teachers, parents, administrators, school board members, and other friends—pay $5.00 to have their signatures embroidered on the banner beneath the logo. By filling in every piece on both sides of the pattern, they hope to raise $1,000 to generate matching funds for special curriculum projects. Rosetta Burr's Friendship Quilt (see figure 97) and the Shadows Quilt (see C-12 in color section) show two patchwork patterns well suited for signature quilts.

Because celebrity-signature quilts appreciate rapidly in value, they have become a favorite auction item. A simple patchwork pattern usually is chosen; then celebrities are invited to sign an actual patch of the background fabric that has been mailed to them. Once returned, their signatures are embroidered, and the quilt blocks assembled.

11. Hat City Quilt.

Our Celebrity Signature Quilt [see C-13 in color section] was made as a fundraiser for our church's new organ and auctioned at a church arts festival. Finding a book in the university library that lists the addresses of famous people, we concentrated on musicians' autographs and found they brought good publicity to the festival and lasting value to the buyer of the quilt.

Janet Aronson, Coventry, Connecticut

Groups have made such quilts using local as well as national celebrities. Does your city have a beloved sports team? How about local political figures or media personalities? A broadened definition of "celebrity" produces many possibilities.

Almost every group that regularly quilts together takes time occasionally to make a raffle quilt. Perhaps they need funds to cover the expenses of a guild quilt show. Some quilts are designed for display, in order to bring new members and publicity, rather than funds, to the group. The Hat City Quilters of Danbury, Connecticut, have used their Hat City Quilt (figure 11) to publicize many of their activities; the Bowers Museum Quilt (figure 12) was originally made to promote displays at the museum and the museum store; while the Weathervane Quilt (figure 13) was raffled among its makers.

When there is plenty of lead time, some groups use the making of a raffle quilt as an opportunity to learn a new quiltmaking technique. For example, the Eastern Long Island Quilter's Guild, raising funds for a quilt show and for scholarships for art students at a nearby college, tried quilt-as-you-go (in which individual blocks are layered, basted, and quilted before being joined) on a traditional appliqué sampler (see C-14 in color section). Another approach was taken by the Summer Hill Quilters in initiating the Bill O'Donnell Memorial Fund at the Johns Hopkins Oncology Center. Theirs was a whitework quilt that was candlewicked and embroidered, with each square designed and worked by members of the group, resulting in many hours of individual work as well as their usual fellowship around the quilting frame (figure 14). As Dorothy Patrick Harris of Phoenix, Maryland, tells it,

Bill had been a local media celebrity, announcing Oriole baseball games prior to his death from

12. Bowers Museum Quilt.

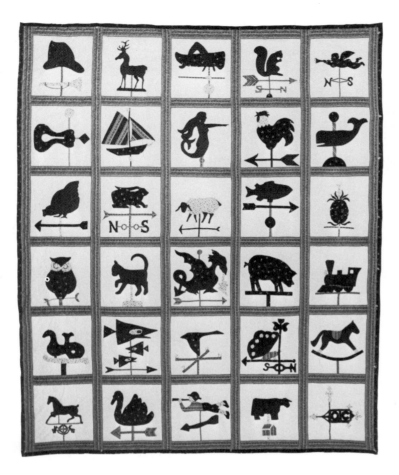

13 (left). Weathervane Quilt.

14 (above). **Summer Hill Quilters** making the Bill O'Donnell Memorial Quilt.

cancer, and Pat, his wife, is a member of our group. We decided to make a raffle quilt after Pat described the frustration of a Hopkins doctor who could not get the funds she needed to buy a small computer to aid her cancer research. We all wanted to do something to let Pat know how much we loved her, mourned her loss, and agreed with her that Johns Hopkins should have the equipment. Because Bill was so well known, it now appears that the memorial fund may become a major charitable cause.

There are, of course, many other groups that were originally formed for the purpose of making fund-raising quilts. Some have represented a one-time effort, resulting in such projects as the Sanibel and Marine Mammal quilts (see C-15 and C-16 in color section). But other groups have continued to make one or more quilts each year. The Caroline Lily Quilt (see C-17 in color section) was made by the Brooktondale, New York, quilting group (figure 15) to be raffled at the annual apple festival. Their quilts have become so well known that buyers want to

purchase tickets even before the next quilt has been made. The Congregational Church Women of Portland, Connecticut, have been making quilts together since 1975, primarily to raise funds at their annual fair. The group started with two dozen members and narrowed down, after several years, to a nucleus of an active eight. In some years they have made more than eight quilts. One of them, the Mariner's Compass Quilt (figure 16), was inspired by a Jinny Beyer seminar on medallion quilts.

But beware. Making quilts to raffle or sell is often more complicated than are other cooperative quilting projects, and not just because of the additional responsibilities of ticket sales and publicity. Planning a realistic quilt that will appeal to a variety of people, fit many settings and uses, have excellent, durable needlework, *and* be finished by a deadline is not an easy task; sometimes it proves impossible. Nonetheless, it is certain that every dollar raised through making and selling quilts is a dollar well earned.

For more information on fundraising quilts, please refer to the supplement at the back of the book.

15 (above). A Brooktondale Quilters (Brooktondale, New York) quilting bee.

16 (right). Mariner's Compass Quilt.

Social Concerns and Message Quilts

Since about 1982, a growing number of groups across the United States have been making peace quilts. One of the first of these was constructed by 35 Boise, Idaho, citizens whose professional, social, spiritual, and political affiliations varied widely. These people came together in order to address the question of what ordinary individuals could do to avert nuclear holocaust. They decided to take a small but concrete step toward understanding and befriending people in the Soviet Union by making a friendship quilt, since quilting is a traditional American art form, and because they were reaching out in friendship to Soviet citizens. The Soviet Embassy in Washington, D.C., helped them send the quilt to the Soviet Women's Committee, which found a permanent home for it in the town of Alitus in Lithuania.

Some members of that original quilt project have joined with others to make the Boise Peace Quilt an ongoing effort. They presented another quilt

(figure 17) to the people of Hiroshima in August 1983 on the anniversary of the bomb blast, and are also collecting nominations for "peacemakers" who will receive an honorary quilt. Norman Cousins, Pete Seeger, and Helen Caldicott have each earned this award.

For us the quilts represent a way to shake off our lethargy and fears and find a way to act. We chose to identify and celebrate positive contributions to the search for peace. We have no illusion that this one small effort—or any other single action—can make the difference between war and peace. But small efforts accumulate like blades of grass to make a meadow, like drops of rain to make a sea.
Deborah Haynes and Diane Jones, Boise, Idaho

The California Marine Mammal Center, located near the Golden Gate Bridge, rescues, treats, and

17. No More Hiroshimas Peace Quilt.

studies distressed marine mammals. Over 150 volunteers work with the professional staff to accomplish the center's main goal: to return stranded marine mammals healthy and wild to their natural habitats along the California coast. Since the center depends on individual memberships and donations from private sources, the staff is continually searching for innovative, successful ways to promote awareness of ocean life and to bring attention to the work of the center. Volunteers decided to make a quilt that would do just this (see C-16 in color section).

Over 60 marine-mammal artists, appliqué specialists, and quilters worked for nine months to create an award-winning group quilt in honor of the center. It pictures 30 different species of marine mammals, and will be exhibited widely in aquariums and marine centers. Posters, postcards, and holiday cards of it will be sold. The skill and spirit evident in the quiltmakers' efforts truly symbolize the center's volunteer spirit and energetic work. It expresses immense appreciation of the beauty of these magnificent marine animals and will gain support for the preservation of life in our oceans.

Peigin Barrett, Fort Cronkhite, California

The makers of the Marine Mammal Quilt benefited from the earlier experience of the Audubon Society group that made the Mono Lake Quilt (see C-18 in color section). As Helen Green of Berkeley, California, tells us,

The Mono Lake Quilt was made to help raise money for legal suits against the City of Los Angeles Department of Water and Power, which has been draining Mono Lake—a saline lake on the east side of the Sierra Nevada Mountains—since 1940. The lake itself and the birds that nest there have been seriously threatened, so our Golden Gate Audubon Conservation Committee started a yearlong fundraising drive. The quilt depicts the flora and fauna of the Mono Basin, which includes the Sierra, Mono Lake, and Tufa Towers area. It was designed by my brother, Ric Hugo, who is a newspaper artist. We grew up on the east side of the Sierras not far from the lake, so the issue is a special one for us. The overall fundraising for Mono Lake eventually brought about $40,000, of which $6,700 was from the quilt. Making the quilt and raffling it took the most

time and energy and was probably a hard way to make $6,700. Because of this experience, our colleagues at the Marine Mammal Center have decided not simply to raffle their quilt, but to use it in a variety of ways to raise funds.

Women inside and outside the California Institution for Women, a prison in Frontera, California, worked together to create a quilted wallhanging (detail, figure 18) describing the personal lives of inmates. The project, sponsored by L.A. Theatre Works with funding from the California Arts Council and the state Department of Corrections, provided two textile artists, Susan Hill and Terry Blecher, to coordinate the workshop and teach needlework skills. Both of these artists had participated previously in Judy Chicago's *Dinner Party*, a massive work of art that incorporated needlework by many women and men, Susan Hill as head of needlework and Terry Blecher as a principal textile artist. Many of the "outside" women who participated in the prison project, titled Texture of Fab-

18. Texture of Fabric—Texture of Life; detail of central panel.

ric—Texture of Life, had worked on or been inspired by the cooperative effort that had produced *Dinner Party*. As Susan and Terry put it,

The final form and content of the quilts did not emerge full-blown right from the beginning, but evolved gradually during the first months of the project. A great deal of time was spent getting to know one another, considering what could be made, and where it could be hung. A long-term cooperative venture was new to many people who "checked us out," and our purpose and generosity were tested. We also needed time to develop people's trust in their own artistic impulses, and for them to trust our ability to appreciate and expand their sensibilities. Eventually, we found that encouraging people to make a standard-format 10-inch quilt block with an original image of their choice provided the enthusiasm needed to carry the project forward. Gradually, imbalances in authority, skill, and responsibility lessened and a fully cooperative group emerged. The final design showed three panels: the women's personal lives as the center panel, with life "outside" and "prison life" on either side. It was unanimously decided that we would go all out to create a beautiful, approachable work that in itself would invite people to notice and challenge the public's view of women in prison. We felt that recognition beyond the personal sphere was very important. It was an essential reason for the insistence on excellent work and clearly articulated themes.

Asian refugee families were the focus of a quilting effort in Washington state. Prior to the quilting classes, the refugees had been helped to find homes and jobs and introduced to the area's history and services. Language lessons also were given.

I'd see the women in the grocery store. They would have trouble remembering what they had learned in language class, or perhaps they were too timid to speak. So a group from four local churches decided we would teach them to quilt so they could practice their English in a more comfortable setting. Boy, did someone learn something, and it wasn't the Asian women! They were expert needleworkers, and they could quilt circles around us. At one point, 9 Asian mothers and their 13 children were attending. We sure did have fun.

Geraldine Lawrence, Centralia, Washington

The Point Richmond, California, PTA raises between $700 and $1,000 each year for the elementary school by making a raffle quilt. One year, members from the PTA, the League of Women Voters, and the East Bay Heritage Quilters who supported Kathy Lord's school-board campaign combined forces to make a raffle quilt (figure 19). Rosemary Corbin of Point Richmond reports that the candidate took it with her to coffees and other campaign gatherings, and someone always sold raffle tickets:

The quilt generated a good deal of publicity, raised $1,800 for Kathy's expenses, and enabled people to make a small contribution to her campaign. Any campaign needs fundraisers at different levels in order to reach all potential donors. The quiltmakers were delighted when she won the election and later became the chairperson of the board.

The Glastonbury (Connecticut) Piecemakers, a quilting group affiliated with the Greater Hartford Quilt Guild, completed this service project for a town-operated home for elderly men after learning of the home's need for new blankets.

We asked our members to donate six-inch squares of fabric that we separated into color groups, laying out a brown random-pattern top on my family-room floor, a blue diagonal Sunshine and Shadow in the living room, and a green top on the porch. Another member donated a top pieced by her grandmother, who had run a boarding house, made from pieces of men's shirts. How appropriate that this quilt should be used, so many years later, by the men at Still Hill! Three other quilts were made, and we delivered all seven, each folded and tied with a bow, just before Christmas. I don't think any of us will forget the warmth we felt that day. The holiday season was rushed; none of us finished everything we had planned. But no one minded because our work for the men at Still Hill was the essence of the holidays for us that year.

Sue Wilder, Glastonbury, Connecticut

19 (opposite). Kathy Lord Campaign Quilt.

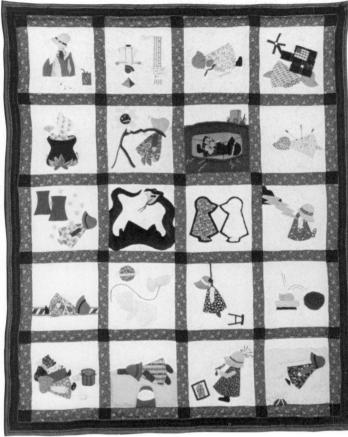

20 (left). Religious Symbols Quilt.

21 (right). The Sun Sets On Sunbonnet Sue. (copyright Seamsters Union Local #500, Lawrence, Kansas, 1979).

In 25 cities across the United States are Ronald McDonald Houses® near children's hospitals, where families of seriously ill children can sleep and support each other while their children are hospitalized. One woman's decision to contribute a quilt to the Milwaukee, Wisconsin, Ronald McDonald House led to a much wider participation by many quilters throughout Wisconsin to provide quilts for all the beds in the house.

I called up to offer one quilt, and the local McDonald's representative agreed it would be a wonderful way to create a more homelike atmosphere. He recognized the value and love contained within a quilt and the importance it could play in uplifting the spirits of parents staying in the house. I felt so good making my quilt that soon I was convincing my many quilting friends to make others. Before I knew it, I had volunteered to gather 50 bed quilts, 12 crib quilts, and wallhangings for the main rooms.

It's upsetting to me that capable quilters some-

times decide not to help because they fear these quilts will receive unusually hard wear. My feeling is that these quilts will indeed be working very hard—to comfort the mother or father of a seriously ill child. When these parents enter their bedroom for the evening, it is the one place where they will find themselves alone—alone with their thoughts, worries, and cares for their child. This is the time they will see the quilts, made as a gift for them by someone who cared, and they will know they are not alone. It's that thought that keeps me working on this project.

Elinor Czarnecki, Cudahy, Wisconsin

Certainly *every* quilt makes a statement, and the purposes of its makers are sewn into every stitch. Friendship quilts say, "We love you" or "We miss you." Raffle quilts say, "We believe in our organization" or "We feel our children need better learning equipment and exciting playgrounds." A quilt picturing flora and fauna of a barrier island (see C-15 in color section) says, "We value our natural environment," and the Religious Symbols Quilt pictured in figure 20 says, "We value our religious heritage." The quilt showing Sunbonnet Sue in shockingly *un*traditional poses (figure 21) says, "We need to take ourselves less seriously as quilters," and pokes fun at our tendency toward habit and cliché.

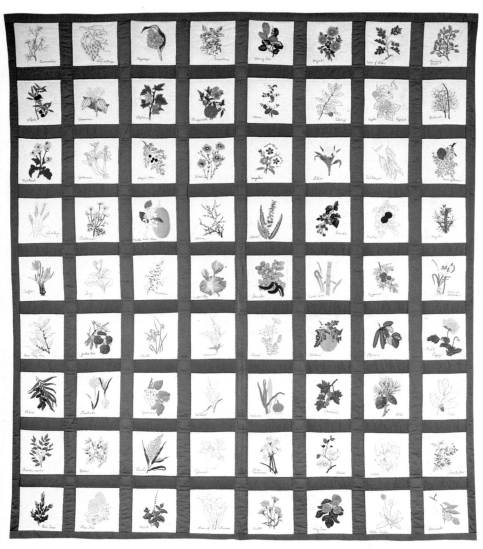

C-1 *Lower right:* Hecht Wedding Quilt.

C-2 *Upper left:* Flowers of the Bible.

C-3 *Lower left:* Ferndale Heritage Quilt.

C-4 *Upper right:* Lote House Quilt.

C-5 *Upper right:* Houses.

C-6 *Lower right:* Beyer Beware.

C-7 *Upper left:* Putnam County Quilt.

C-8 The Great Things About Pittsburgh Quilt.

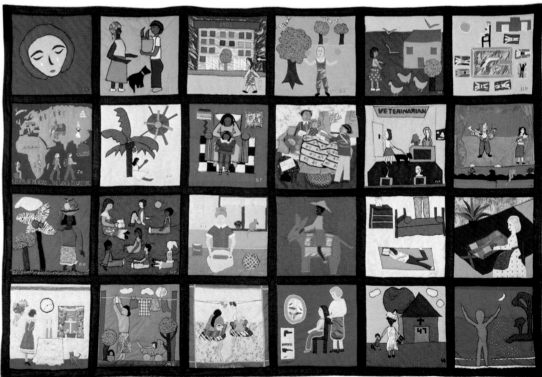

C-9 *Upper left:* Baltimore Culture and Heritage: Past, Present, and Future (copyright, Summer Hill Quilters, 1981).

C-10 *Upper right:* Washington Perspective (copyright, Capitol Quilters, 1982).

C-11 *Lower right:* Cambridge Women's Quilt.

C-12 *Lower right:* Shadows Quilt.

C-13 *Upper right:* Celebrity Signature Quilt.

C-14 *Lower left:* Appliqué Sampler.

C-15 *Upper left:* Sanibel Quilt.

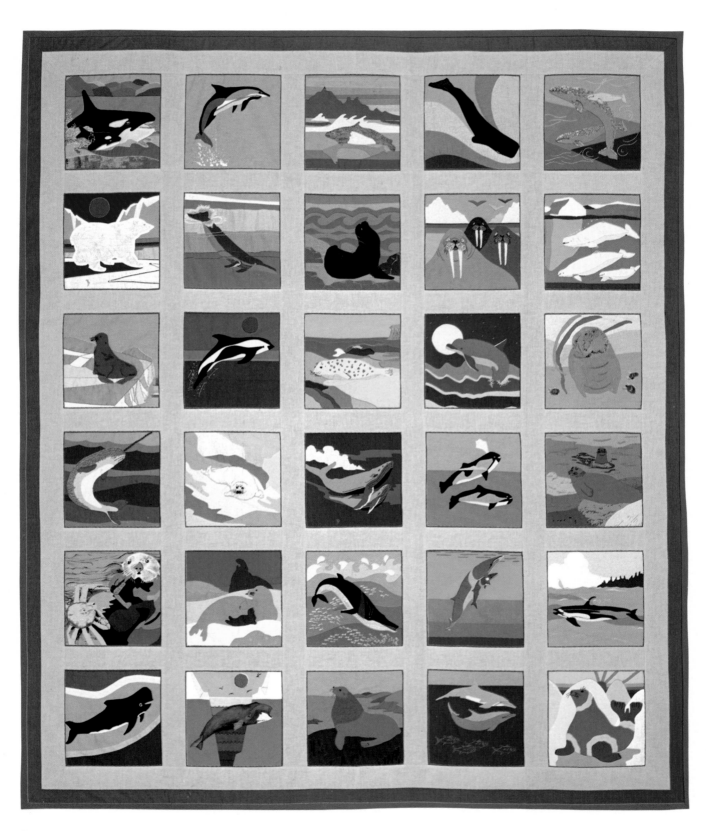

C-16 Marine Mammal Quilt.

C-17 *Upper right:* Caroline Lily.

C-18 *Lower right:* Mono Lake Quilt.

C-19 *Upper left:* Chaplin Elementary School Quilt.

C-20 *Lower left:* Teachers' Centers Quilt.

C-21 *Upper right:* Daisy Chain.

C-22 *Lower right:* Origins.

C-23 *Upper left:* Footlights at Wolf Trap
(copyright, Judy Spahn, 1983).

C-24 *Lower left:* Pueblo Indian Designs.

Like Madame Defarge's knitting, each of these quilts records not only a message but a period of history that is soon to disappear—but not without a trace. Last Sunday night I brought my needle-work with me to a meeting of our local Nuclear Freeze Committee, a potluck supper and sing-along designed to raise money to send one of our members to Washington to lobby for a responsible arms control policy. I was joining the hexagons of my first Grandmother's Flower Garden flower, stitching the petals into place, as a group led us in song.

There was one song I had never heard before, and its haunting chorus went, "Feel the earth. See the sky. Hear our children's children cry." As the sorrow of the lyrics blended with the harmony of our voices, I carefully made a triple knot that would not unravel easily, a knot that seemed to bind me to every woman who had left her needlework behind her to mother future generations. "What are you making?" someone whispered. And suddenly the answer came to me: In the valley of the shadow, I am making a quilt to keep my children's children warm.

Linda Weltner, Marblehead, Massachusetts

Quilts Made by Children

While researching this book we discovered many interesting and exciting quilts made by children. All kinds of quilts have been created with the help of teachers, baby-sitters, and daycare providers. One mother helped her four- and five-year-olds make a story quilt with marker pens one rainy weekend. We learned of imaginative themes for classroom project quilts—favorite animals, hearts, self-portraits (figure 22), local landmarks and local history, hobbies and interests (figure 23), children of many countries, shapes made from paper folding (see C-19 in color section), scenes near the school, favorite stories, sports, alphabets, to name only a few. Some

are designed by children and sewn by adults. Others are made entirely by children. All are reminiscent of pioneer schools, where learning to piece a Nine Patch block was standard third-grade curriculum.

By the time she retired from her work as librarian and quilt club coordinator at a Queens, New York,

---

22 (left). Self-Portraits Quilt.

23 (right). Students at Franklin School, Berkeley, California, quilting High Interest Rate.

24 (above). Quilts made by Jean Linden and students at P.S. 48, Queens, New York.

25 (right). Ben Franklin Quilt.

inner-city school, Jean Linden had made 22 quilts with her elementary school students (figure 24). Some of these quilts have been exhibited at the Department of Education in Washington, D.C. The Ben Franklin Quilt (figure 25) was the school's contribution to the 1976 Bicentennial.

Since our school principal strongly resembles Ben Franklin, and was willing to come dressed as Ben for the occasion, we built our bicentennial celebration around Franklin himself. Our quilt has three types of needlework, in red, white, and blue, and is united by a pieced patchwork design called The Tail of Benjamin's Kite. Appliqué blocks show Franklin's roles as printer, cartoonist, patriot, and scholar. Cross-stitched maxims from *Poor Richard's Almanac* were chosen by the children and stitched through graph paper. How do you like, "Fish and visitors stink after three days?"
Jean Linden, Kew Gardens, New York

Mothers of young children at the Chaplin (Connecticut) Elementary School knew of the students' need for playground equipment. They agreed to make a raffle quilt if the children would do the designing (see C-19 in color section). The reading specialist suggested giving each child a nine-inch square of paper to be folded and then colored in by the children. The resulting designs were faithfully reproduced in patchwork blocks (including one "To Mommy" inscription), as were the colors the children had used. All the original paper squares were preserved in an album that is kept at the school.

In 1982, Miss Albertson was about to retire as principal of the Traver Road School, a position she had held for many years. It was decided that each class would make one quilt-as-you-go block and the PTA parents would do the two presentation blocks for a retirement quilt. Each class would decide on a theme, draw a design on paper, and then transfer it to a muslin block. Then the individual sandwiches would be made and sashing added, after which the

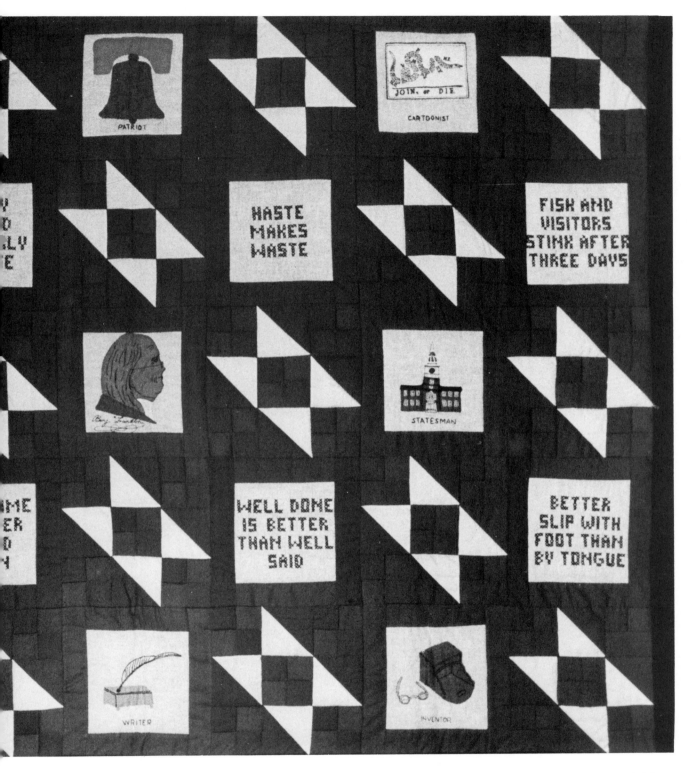

children would quilt the blocks. Ruth Klein of Salt Point, New York, who taught the quilting techniques to the teachers (who in turn taught the children) remembers that

excitement was high as every child participated in their secret gift for "our Miss Albertson." By the end of May all the blocks except the PTA's were finished. To our surprise and relief, each one covered a different aspect of school life. I completed the presentation blocks and then joined them all and bound the quilt. When the 480 children presented the quilt to Miss Albertson, she was overjoyed.

Carol Trimble, a primary classroom teacher in Oakland, California, told us about quilts she made with her kindergarten-through-second-grade students

Her favorite was one of self-portraits made as the last in a series of projects, studies, and experiments her students did about themselves and their bodies. To make the quilt, each child drew him or herself, then chose and cut fabrics for the different areas of the picture. Carol appliquéd the cutouts by machine at home, and the children did all the hand embroidery and finish work. The quilt hung in the auditorium while the class performed to the song "Free to Be You and Me" by Marlo Thomas to culminate their studies of themselves. "It is amazing," Carol reports, "how much each picture is true to how the children saw themselves at that time. I could write reams about what each self-portrait says about its artist. We gave the quilt to the school, and it hangs in the library."

Jane Smith of South Berwick, Maine, teaches junior-high sewing and gets a lot of help from students who are bored during study hall periods: "If they come with nothing to do, I show them how much fun it is to piece patchwork. We always have a Grandmother's Flower Garden or two in the making. They not only learn to sew, but grow to love doing it. Quilting with kids may take a lot of energy on my part and careful planning, but it is certainly worth it!"

Jan Inouye of Berkeley, California, taught her son's 4-5-6th-grade class to quilt. Their theme of hobbies and interests resulted in a quilt called High Interest Rate (figure 23), whose blocks were made by embroidering over felt-tip markers. Jan tells us that the children raffled the quilt among themselves in a very suspenseful and elaborate ceremony. The same class is making another quilt this year, using a resist method for the blocks. "I took them to the East Bay Heritage Quilters show for which I'd put together a worksheet to help them appreciate what they were looking at. I'm just ensuring that the future generation will be full of quilt lovers."

Although we have decided not to include more specific how-tos for working with children, we could not resist a few suggestions—perhaps because we are both former schoolteachers. Any quilt opens a wealth of possibilities for research in many curriculum areas: history, science, geometry, social studies, art and design, as well as the practical skills and tools of writing, printing, editing, measuring, drawing, public speaking, photography, reading, and sewing both by hand and by machine. How were windows made in 1779? How do you draw an oyster? What happens when different colors are placed side by side? How do you enlarge a drawing? What are perspective and scale, symmetry and tesselation? What will the area of the finished quilt be? Who will write a press release about it? Can we get our picture in the newspaper? What should we do to thank the people who helped us, and how shall we celebrate the first hanging of the quilt? There's easily a year's worth of work here. Figure 26 shows a piece of writing that Nederlands, Colorado, sixth-graders prepared and edited for their class book on quilting, which describes one step in the quiltmaking process.

Many people can help with children's quilts: art teachers, nursery school teachers, home economics teachers, extension agents, scout leaders—anyone who has helped children learn to sew. We've found it is better to seek out experts with children rather than expert needleworkers, although often you can find both strengths in the same person. It's important that initial projects be easy, flexible, and geared to be highly successful. Don't turn the children off to needlework by demanding perfect products, or by making the project too difficult for them to finish. If adults do most of the work, the children can

26. A page from a sixth-grade class book about the quilt they made. The copy has been edited and is ready for final typing.

Learning to Embroider

Mrs. Norris (Krystal's mother) came in to help us learn how to embroider. We started on the outline stitch, but some of us had a lot of trouble with it, so we decided to do a running stitch instead.

Each of us took a scrap of material and drew a picture or design in it for practice. The designs turned out great in spite of all the problems we had - sewing them into our shirts, running the needle through a finger instead of the material, and making knots big enough to tie a horse to a hitchin post.

Here is Eddie's practice embroidery.

OK Jeff   OK. Regan   READY TO RETYPE
OK, Danny

hardly feel proud of it or go home with new skills. Children can be very good at helping one another with sewing if they are thoughtfully paired for skills, patience, and kindness. Classroom quilting is definitely a long-term project—one best completed without a deadline, nor limited to Friday afternoons. Once children have learned the basics, they can sew while being read to or during any in-between moments of the school day. Finally, don't miss the opportunity quiltmaking offers to bring new and interested adults into the life of your school—and your own and your children's lives as well.

In every case, parents and teachers worked together, which was a nice side benefit. Many interesting and productive discussions took place over the quilting frame. Sometimes we tried to solve personal, local, or global issues, but whatever we discussed, we got to know each other better and respect each other more.

Rosemary Corbin, Point Richmond, California

Friendship, Gratitude, and Separation Quilts

Is there someone you'd like to honor or thank in a different way? A friend who's changing jobs or having an important birthday? A beloved librarian or baby-sitter, a minister or grandparent? Are there teachers or other mentors who opened doors for you or your children? Many of these important people can be thanked with a quilt made especially for them. Although such a gift may be presented at or prompted by a special event—a birthday, a job change, a move to another city—its main purpose is primarily an expression of the friendship and love that bind the makers and recipients. The Summer Hill Quilters in Phoenix, Maryland, so honored one of their founding members, Leslie Dundore, who moved just as they were celebrating their first success—a $1,000 prize for their first group quilt (see C-9 in color section). Out of love for her they made a coverlet she could take to her new home.

Because these quilts are made to express love, other considerations are secondary. The whole group must be completely accepting of each other's work, for to criticize the work is to reject the love put into making it. Barbara Wysocki of Rocky Hill, Connecticut, deals with the question of acceptance reassuringly in this letter inviting her family to make a cooperative quilt:

I have a special quilt [figure 27] I'd like to make for Nanny, but I need your help. Each of you—child, grandchild, and great-grandchild—will be sent one Sawtooth Star block that I have pieced. All you need to do is put something in the middle that represents you and your family. It could be just your names, significant dates, a picture of your favorite things, or anything that is especially you or that reminds you of Nanny. If you wanted to embroider or permanently Magic Mark it, that would be just fine. I don't expect

great works of art or fabulous needlework—just be sure it won't wash out, shrink, or run. I'd love to hear any ideas you have on how to improve this.

Even people who've never sewn before are often moved by love for the receiver of the quilt to make a uniquely beautiful and carefully crafted piece of work.

Because these quilts represent many shared years in the lives of all the makers, the quilt coordinator may choose a backseat role, encouraging the participants to take on most of the collecting, piecing, documenting, and presenting of the quilt. Careful attention must be given to being *inclusive*. It is good to plan a way to incorporate extra blocks late in the process. The Teachers' Centers Quilt (see C-20 in color section) was designed with blank corner blocks, but by the time it was complete, all four had been filled in and the label moved to the back! Other groups that have had more than the anticipated number of contributors have ended up making another quilt, pillows, or a scrapbook with the extra blocks.

For the sake of friendship, people will often make heroic efforts to bring a quilt into being. Some groups have met one night a week for many months. Others have sent over a thousand letters and cards, as did those who made the Teachers' Centers Quilt. Women at St. Paul's Episcopal Church in Grand Forks, North Dakota, took down the quilting frame (and hid it in a closet) each time the unsuspecting recipient—the rector's wife—came near the building. The women of Grace Lutheran Church in La Grange Park, Illinois, quilted day and night to finish the quilt for their assistant pastor while he was away on a brief vacation (see C-2 in color section). Doris Kampe's friends and fellow needle-

27 (opposite). Nanny's Album Quilt.

28 (left). Doris Kampe Friendship Quilt.

29 (above). Teachers' Centers Quilt; New Haven Teacher Center, Inc., logo block.

workers manufactured months of excuses for not having any new projects to show her while they worked on her friendship quilt (figure 28).

The way a friendship quilt is presented is especially important. A receiver may well prefer to share in your feelings of love and appreciation by participating in the making of the quilt itself. If you think she would enjoy being part of the fellowship of the quilting bees, you might choose to present her with the partially quilted project and invite her to finish it with you.

When historians refer to friendship quilts, they're usually describing either album quilts—in which each block contains a personalized picture—or signature quilts—in which names or signatures appear, often with a unifying theme. The Teachers' Center Quilt, whose label on the back dedicates it to Kathleen Devaney, for eight years the director of a na-

tional networking service for teachers' centers, is a type of signature quilt, since about a third of its blocks are different centers' logos (figure 29 shows one of them).

Another type of signature quilt is described by Jeanette Johnson of Pineville, Louisiana:

Several years ago I began thinking about making a family friendship quilt, but the idea only came alive at my mother's 85th birthday celebration. After that I decided to "fish or cut bait"—to do it now or forget it forever. The squares have a design of a bird and a flower with space in the center for a name, town, and birthdate. Each woman in our family completed her square using her own choice of color and stitch. My mother was born in 1886, the last granddaughter in 1980, and there is a female born in each decade between those dates. When I finished quilting it, I embroidered this information on the border: "Family members embroidered each square for Jeanette, who designed and made this quilt June 1979–August 1980."

Another intergenerational quilt was made by the families of the eleven children of the Reverend Jesse Edward Rolston and Ada Leah Rolston as part of their third family reunion—which 110 family members attended. Each of the 12 blocks pictures significant places, events, people, and interests in the Rolston family history. Today the quilt hangs in the original family home in Sheldon, Iowa.

Many quilters have mourned a loss through the ritual of making a quilt. The very act of quilting reflects an approach to life and healing that one needs in times of distress: one stitch at a time; one patch at a time; one day at a time. The makers can take as long as they like to create the quilt, but there is often an unspoken assumption that by the time they finish it, they too will be ready to move on from their grieving.

My dear friends were moving to Israel. We were all part of a group that meets to celebrate Shabbat and holidays. I wanted us to do something special for them—a friendship quilt. The idea for my own block came all in one piece. The words were "For everything there is a season," and the picture, a tree with the seasons changing around the branches and the Hebrew word *chai*, which means "life," embroidered into the bark.

I took the quilt top with me on a boat trip. Each day I quilted another block, saving my own for last. On the final day of vacation I completed the quilt. It was with great sadness that I sewed the stitches, realizing that the summer was ending and that the time for final good-byes was imminent. For me, making the quilt was an important part of the leave-taking—my personal separation ritual.

My friends have moved many times in Israel, but they write that wherever they are, the quilt hangs proudly on their wall. For them it is a tangible reminder of friends and wonderful times shared. It is also their way of sharing us with their 18-month-old son as they tell him about each picture and its creator.

Helene Sapadin, New Haven, Connecticut

But a friendship quilt is likely to be at least as comforting for the receiver as it was for its makers, as Barbara Wysocki found with the quilt she put together with her family for her grandmother:

When I'd been quilting for a year I decided to make my first large quilt [figure 27] for my grandmother—we called her Nanny. She was living in a nursing home in New Jersey, and I wanted to personalize the room for her. [The invitation Barbara sent to her family to make blocks for this quilt is at the beginning of this section.] Our family is spread from Connecticut to California, so I was the only grandchild able to visit her regularly. I knew she missed her family, and they certainly missed her. This is the letter I wrote to all the family after we delivered the quilt to her in February:

It was so exciting to receive each of your special, individual blocks. They showed thought, planning, and most of all love for Nanny. I joined them together and put the quilt in the frame, aiming for a completion date near Nanny and Pappy's wedding anniversary in February. I quilted daily—sometimes with the kids close by, sometimes with Bernie asleep a few feet away. As it began to take shape, I could see the quilt was all I'd hoped it would be. Then I copied some excerpts from your letters, attached some pictures, and made them into a small booklet. On February 17, Susy and I drove to North Jersey with our precious cargo. Nanny's reaction was quiet astonishment. Her hands slid gently over the blocks and border as she looked from one square to the next. She was just enjoying the experience of holding it, just like holding all of you. I showed her who had made each block, but most of the time she knew before I got to it. Then we laid it on her bed—a perfect fit. Her pride was obvious as she'd say to each passing nurse and friend, "Come see what my family made me." She saved the booklet to read—like a special dessert when you're full from a good meal. The quilt is a gift she sees and touches every day, and in that way she has us all near her always.

Whenever we visited her during the next ten months the quilt was always on her bed. Early in November she became ill, and when we came to see her she was in bed, obviously dying. Two days later she died quietly, still covered with the quilt. Though she was alone I've always felt she knew that her family was with her.

Designing the Cooperative Quilt

The quilts made today are a far cry from their traditional ancestors. We have seen quilts made of paper and plastic, quilts made with clothes-dryer lint, and quilts fashioned to look like ears of corn, pancakes, and dog houses. Some fabrics have been hand woven, some elaborately dyed and over-dyed with chemical or natural dyes. Quilt surfaces have been painted, embellished with all manner of stitchery, and subjected to the technological wizardry of photographic transfer processes. This fantastic parade of artistry continues to amaze and amuse us, providing us with new ideas for our own projects. Novel media like silk screen or fabric crayons provide us with alternatives to sewing that may help to include nonsewers in our projects (figures 30 and 31). In spite of all the modern alternatives, however, patchwork and appliqué remain the favorite quiltmaking techniques, and choosing to design one or the other will be one of your first decisions.

Patchwork vs Appliqué

Appliqué is the art of sewing motifs or patches to a backing fabric to form pictures, graphic symbols, or even words. Because of this pictorial quality, appliqué provides an ideal medium for direct communication. Messages to the world can be delivered via appliqué quilts as various as the messengers themselves, ranging from the sentimental (figure 6: "I left my heart in San Francisco") to open protest (figure 21: "We're sick of Sunbonnet Sue!"). Quilts, unusually flexible vehicles for conveying human emotion, often tell a good deal about the quiltmakers, and the love, pride, humor, pain, and sadness that went into their pictures.

Anyone can make appliqué quilts, but the work of beginners is apt to have a rather primitive charm.

Experienced hand sewers will be able to appliqué sharp points and graceful curves with nearly invisible stitches, but even advanced seamstresses will find appliqué more time-consuming than patch-

Appliqué quilts present a few structural considerations, as well. If the quilt is for a bed or for a baby, the fabrics must be much more durable than if the quilt is to be a wall hanging. Appliqué quilts invite uneven stitching, and they often incorporate small pieces that may not stay attached during normal use. Appliqué blocks must be set right side up, which means that such a quilt cannot be rotated on the bed to allow it to wear evenly.

By contrast, patchwork blocks often appear equally interesting when viewed sideways or upside

30 (top). Bunce Family
Anniversary Quilt;
Jim Payne's block.

31 (bottom). Bunce Family
Anniversary Quilt;
Sarah's block.

down. This practical feature enables patchwork bed quilts to survive to ripe old ages, even when in continuous use. Many antique quilts are square, not because beds were square then, but because the quilt could be turned to wear all the edges evenly.

Patchwork, or pieced, quilts are made of precisely cut shapes of fabric sewn to each other to form the quilt surface. The unique beauty of patchwork quilts lies in their geometric intricacy and precision. Line, color, and texture combine and recombine to create surfaces that appeal to our intuitive natures. Three-dimensional illusions frequent this two-dimensional plane, surprising and delighting us. Pieced quilts, whether antique reproductions or contemporary styles, can be sewn by machine or by hand. The stitches are hidden on the wrong side of the quilt top, so even a beginner can produce tolerably good blocks. Patchwork designs are available in an infinite variety, from simple to intricate, and usually these designs can be pieced quickly. If your group chooses to work a pieced quilt, you will be following a distinctively American tradition, one that stirs us to romantic thoughts of simpler days when quilts were often the only artistic outlet for a woman.

Selecting Fabric

The favored choice for patchwork is 100 percent cotton fabric, prewashed to remove extra dye and sizing. Cotton's natural fiber eases or stretches to accommodate small errors in piecing. When pressed with a warm iron, it obediently lies flat. And it is available in an enticing range of colors and prints.

The Propeller Quilt (figure 118, in the pattern section), incorporates a great many different cotton fabrics. A committee chose unbleached muslin and a green print for the key fabrics. These were divided and distributed with the request that each quilter supply coordinating fabrics from her own scrap-bag to piece the rest of her block. The key fabrics provide unity; the scraps, variety and texture. In Judy Martin's Daisy Chain (see C-21 in color section), the off-white background provides a similar foil for the various scrap-bag fabrics that create the chain.

Today's almost unlimited selection of fabrics can cause some problems for quilters, too. Fabric manufacturers, well aware of the ready market for quilting textiles, have been producing collections of closely coordinated fabrics. These seductive fabrics look beautiful together while they are still on the bolts. Nonetheless, once your quilt blocks have been cut and sewn, these fabrics prove to be so similar in scale and hue that they melt into each other, destroying the "pieced" look that is the very essence of patchwork. When these same closely coordinated fabrics are made into appliqué quilts, they result in a slick, homogenized look that is likely to sell your design short.

Appliqué invites the use of a wide range of fabrics with varying textures, well beyond the traditional cottons, especially if the quilt is to be a wall hanging. Many women are scrap savers, and when a call for odd bits of fabric goes out, the response is apt to be overwhelming. Mary Potts Montgomery of Oberlin, Ohio, reports that when her group formed a communal pile of fabric scraps, one meeting consisted of going through it in good bargain-basement style. "Fabric suddenly took on new qualities and possibilities. Ann decided that her son's old striped jeans would be perfect for Peter Pindar Pease's log cabin. Sabra was wearing a jumper that seemed ideal for making brick walks and buildings—luckily, there were scraps available!"

But beware. Although the use of a wide variety of fabrics in a quilt can add to its originality, some of these fabrics may present such problems as fraying, stretching, or transparency. Again, the easiest fabric to work with is 100 percent cotton; it is closely woven and does not fray when cut. When quilters choose from different supplies of fabric, the quilt will sometimes have an unrelated, hodgepodge look, not unified enough to be aesthetically pleasing. This problem can be solved by choosing fabrics from a common pool or by careful selection of sashing and borders. Purchasing the sashing fabric ahead of time and giving a snippet to each participant will help the sewers keep the overall color scheme in mind. When their quilts feature outdoor scenes, some groups unify them by purchasing sky blue and grass green fabrics and giving these to each quilter.

We have also seen a number of appliqué quilts without *enough* variety in color or fabric. Inexperienced quilters are sometimes timid, especially when given a blank square of unbleached muslin and no guidelines. Novice quilters need samples, suggestions, or ideas about what fabrics to choose and what colors would be appropriate.

Personalizing Blocks

The use of many fabrics coupled with pictorial freedom allow appliqué quilts to be highly individualistic. If appropriate in your quilt, personalizing the blocks will make it that much more special.

Many personal touches crept into the quilt. For instance, the McGrath block was redesigned by a woman whose 35-year-old husband had recently died of a heart attack. In previous years, he had been part of the Iditarod "Air Force"—volunteer pilots who fly the trail to drop off food, return dropped dogs to Nome or Anchorage, and spot mushers along the way. The airplane in the block is his—his colors, his number on the tail.

In another instance, I was working on the Anchorage block after the first mushers had arrived in Nome. Mushers are housed by local people, and one of my mushing guests, Susan Butcher, was looking over my shoulder as I worked. When I realized that my block needed a musher in it, she suggested, "Give it number 3," (her number this year). She then selected fabric for the parka, and I completed it by giving the figure long braids. She was delighted, and everyone who looks at the quilt says, "That's Susan Butcher!"

Stephanie Barnett, Nome, Alaska

The appliqué quilt Nancy Hoffmann's group in Philadelphia made offered different sorts of personal contributors:

The old magnolia trees that are part of our Victorian neighborhood served as a starting point for the central medallion. Around it, individuals pieced the leaded glass windows in their homes or other items that suggest Victorian themes. The four corner squares are patchwork renditions of the brick paving in the neighborhood.

Patchwork quilts can be personalized, too. Mary Ann Spencer coordinated an origins quilt (see C-22 in color section) personalized with both pieced blocks and quilting designs.

Each block depicts an aspect of the heritage of this area of northern California. Eureka, in Humbolt County, is a rural coastal town with lumber and fishing as its principal economic resources. So patchwork blocks were chosen for their names: Log Cabin, Birds in the Air, Bear's Paw, Ocean Wave, Carpenter's Wheel, Fish, and so on. Our Indian heritage inspired us to develop two blocks with designs from museum Indian baskets. Even the quilting pattern in the sashing is taken from the geometric shape of the concrete blocks used to reinforce our harbor.

Hand vs. Machine Sewing

Appliqué is almost always done by hand (see the end of this chapter for appliqué directions), but some people are skilled at machine appliqué. If a group member is a virtuoso with her zigzag satin stitch, you may be able to design the project so the quilters learn this technique. Pattie Chase and Susan Thompson taught machine appliqué as part of the process when they helped create the Cambridge Women's Quilt (see C-11 in color section), so this masterwork combines both hand and machine appliqué.

Pieced blocks are often sewn by machine, but

even when pieced by hand, patchwork is faster than appliqué. Quilters quickly develop preferences for hand or machine sewing. Ideally, your project will provide both kinds of opportunities, perhaps with hand-pieced or hand-appliquéd blocks and machine-sewn sashing, borders, and binding.

In cooperative situations, quilting is best done by hand. Machine quilting is difficult to do well, and it is a job for only one person. Hand quilting affords the comraderie of sitting at a large frame to work with others, an experience that many consider the best part of the whole project.

Designing the Appliqué Quilt

Whether simple or complex, your appliqué quilt will require thoughtful planning. You will need to consider what subjects to picture, where to place them on the quilt, and how to render them in fabric. Sets, sashes, and borders, which frame the quilt and unify the design, must be planned. Let's consider some of the special design challenges that appliqué presents.

ONE SCENE OR MANY?

The most common way to design appliqué quilts is block by block, each person coming up with her own design for her own block. This fine traditional method of construction was used for the Marine Mammal and The Great Things About Pittsburgh quilts (see C-16 and C-8 in color section). Scenic quilts—those with one overall picture—are most often designed by one person and usually are highly stylized, as are the Hecht Wedding and Mono Lake quilts (see C-1 and C-18 in color section). One person's vision for the quilt is realized by the others, who make sections of it. The Putnam County Quilt (see C-7 in color section), designed by Gladys Boalt, is one of these. Notice the way the native floral and animal borders frame the scenes, separate the sections, and at the same time provide unity.

IDEAS FOR PICTURES

Whether your quilt is designed block by block or put together in sections as a single scene, you will need a source of pictorial ideas for your appliqués. We believe such sources are all around us, especially in our ordinary daily lives (figures 32, 33, and 34). Julie Morrison from Glens Falls, New York, also found this to be true.

In 1976 I was given a friendship quilt. Twelve friends each designed an appliqué picture that reflected some special experience each person had shared with me: learning to ski together, taking our children to the kindergarten bus, helping at Head Start. The amazing thing is, two of the women do no sewing, and only two of them had done any quilting. The quilting stitches are those of beginners, but the designs are priceless to me.

We have seen several hundred pictorial appliqué quilts, and the ones we find most appealing are those in which the pictures have particular meaning to the people involved. These designs are not only special to those who made them, but also inspire curiosity in the casual viewer, drawing a different sort of attention.

A number of historical appliqué patterns (notably Lancaster Rose and her many Rose cousins, and the Sunbonnet folks, Sue and Sam) have made the transition to the last quarter of the twentieth century. These can be appealing, beautiful patterns, like the ones used in the Appliqué Sampler (see C-14 in color section). But traditional appliqués may lack the magnetic quality of personalized blocks, and they have a built-in hazard: They have a way of becoming trite, inviting the kind of parody we see in The Sun Sets on Sunbonnet Sue (figure 21). Our hope is that you will take inspiration from these pages and create your own appliqué patterns. Toward that end, we include here a number of photos of appliqué quilts, suggestions on how to make your own appliqués, and general directions for stitching. Books by Virginia Avery and Jean Ray Laury are helpful to those who are interested in more on appliqué (see Resources in back of book).

32. Herb Society Quilt; Onion block (logo of the Northern Illinois Herb Society Unit).

33 (right). Doris Kampe Friendship Quilt;
Ball Jar block.

34 (below). Doris Kampe Friendship Quilt;
Raspberries block.

DRAWING PROBLEMS

For many of us, our drawing careers ended in early elementary school, and even today when we are asked to sketch, we somehow instantly warp back to our eighth year and produce stick-figure people playing near lollipop trees under a yellow-ball sun. Yet in the fertile recesses of our minds, our fantasies create splendid realistic, colorful pictures for our quilts. How can we approximate these visionary appliqués when our drawing skills seem to have stopped short at grade three?

Successful designs do not flow freely from the pencils of even skilled artists; they evolve gradually. The key to designing appliqué pictures is simplicity. Reduce your drawing to its basic components, eliminating fussy details. The final drawing should look like those in preschool coloring books—clean and simple. Even if you take liberties with reality, your appliqué will still be successful as long as the characteristic features of your subject are included. Think about what few things really identify your subject, and picture these things in your block. Details can be embroidered, drawn with liquid embroidery pens, or painted.

To this end, we would like to encourage you to try three things that have worked for others: (1) helping one another through using the talent in the group; (2) working out your own designs with the help of an artist-teacher; or (3) working with mechanical copy aids.

WORKING WITH THE TALENT IN THE GROUP

Everyone in your group has some talent to offer, and we have often found that design problems can be resolved by the group as a whole. This process works best when you have shown some faith in the project by bringing your ideas and a beginning sketch to the group. No one appreciates a Helpless Hannah who expects others to completely lay out her block for her. On the other hand, if you want help or need advice on your design, be sure to present it to the group while it is still roughed out and easy to change. If your block already looks finished, people will be reluctant to suggest renovations.

Quilt teacher Mary Coyne Penders of Vienna, Virginia, discovered how vital it was for her students to pool their resources:

It was soon apparent that our undertaking was far more time consuming than originally envisioned by my advanced-class brochure, and that the tasks involved in developing the designs were too complex for the class. Then the group process came into focus, as each of the nine turned to one another for advice and support. Soon they were exchanging tasks and participating in one another's artwork. People who could not draw found themselves learning to do so. Those who were uncertain about color and fabric selection found themselves in decision-making situations with the whole group an instant support system. Individual strengths were enlarged, weaknesses overcome. Class members gained self-confidence along with new skills and techniques.

As a teacher, I was able to progress from facilitator and arbiter to agent of change. Slowly, the dependency relationship of this class changed as they became their own teachers as well as learners.

Cathy Smith in Chaplin, Connecticut, found much the same to be true from her vantage point as group member:

Each had something different to offer. One woman had a beautiful sense of color that inspired us all, another drew butterflies to be quilted on the background squares, another was extremely precise and made us cringe about all those loose

35. Cambridge Women's Quilt; working together on the Take Back the Night block.

threads we had failed to trim off, and so on for each member. Besides giving time, energy, and talent to the project, we all came away with an awareness of other members' needs and talents that would never have occurred if we had not made the quilt.

WORKING WITH AN ARTIST

Some of the quilts in this book were designed by artists. Although we do not have to be artists to design beautiful quilts, there is much to learn from these masterworks about how to plan our own projects so that they are consistent in scale and imaginative in color and fabric choices. An artist thinks about the quilt as a whole—how would it look hanging on a wall? An artist is not concerned about the individual blocks, except as they relate to the whole quilt. Quiltmakers, on the other hand, tend to lavish their concern on each individual block, losing the overview in the process. This is like the old forest-and-trees problem; if each tree is hale and hearty but the entire forest is planted in the path of the new interstate highway, disappointment will lie ahead when you finally see the larger picture. You'll save yourself a lot of "transplanting" by maintaining that artistic, "wholistic" vision as your group plans the individual blocks.

If envisioning the quilt and drawing the designs proves to be a real problem for a group, it may be worthwhile to work with an artist. Some quilt co-ordinators have given the job to one or more artists, as was the case with the California Marine Mammal Center's quilt (see C-16 in color section), for which professionals donated drawings. If you do work with an artist, be sure that he or she clearly understands how appliqués are made, otherwise the drawings may be too detailed to render in fabric.

Rather than having the artist do the drawings for you, why not have her serve as advisor, working with each of you as you design your own block? If no one volunteers for this job, the art teacher at your local school could be drafted for an evening in exchange for quilting lessons, or some other creative barter item, or perhaps a cash stipend. This seems like one of the best uses of an artist's talents, and also becomes most rewarding for the artist herself, serving as teacher, sharing her knowledge, and bringing out your latent talent.

Although the group was composed of women of all ages, many of whom had never met each other before the project began, a comraderie quickly developed as one volunteer with a specific talent assisted another. For instance, Marcia Carpenter, an artist and shopkeeper in Chester's craft village

36 (left). **Dayton Historical Houses; Peabody Hill block.**

37 (right). **Dayton Historical Houses; First Baptist Church block.**

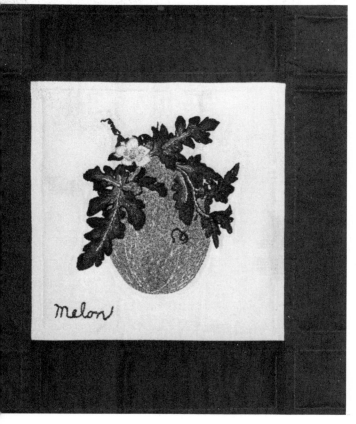

of Sugar Loaf, sketched the design for the quilt square that Rose Laroe, an octogenarian, was doing, while Rose showed those who had never quilted before how to do basic stitches.

Patricia Edwards Clyne, Chester, New York

WORKING WITH VISUAL AIDS

Even without professional help, you can do a great deal yourself. If you are working on scenes or buildings, take a color slide of your subject and project it on the wall. Trace around the image, eliminating fussy details. This technique was used in the Dayton Historical Houses blocks (figures 36 and 37). Opaque projectors will project a print or instant-camera picture onto a wall. Graph paper is a handy aid for designing architectural structures and cityscapes. Do all of your architectural blocks at the same time to be sure that the scale is consistent.

Don't forget copying. Photocopying from books is a legitimate way to *learn*. If the quilt is to be sold or displayed, however, you must obtain the artist's permission to use the design. (Artists may be contacted through the publication in which you saw their work.) The women who created the Sanibel Quilt (See C-15 in color section) live on a beautiful island in the Gulf of Mexico. Although they are not artists themselves, they admired the work of naturalists Charles Harper and Ikki Matsumoto, who granted the quilters permission to use their designs, and this collaboration produced stunning results. In another instance, Jackie Dodson used embroidered flowers taken from Winifred Walker's *All the Plants of the Bible* in the quilt (see C-2 in color section) that she coordinated (details in figures 38 and 39). The Point Richmond PTA appropriately used illustrations from popular children's books for their 1982 raffle quilt (see figure 8).

When creating designs for appliqué, your imagination is your best ally. If things are not perfect, have a good laugh and consider your quilt a real original.

As work progressed, we became familiar with the hassles and headaches connected with each block: the taffeta church steeple that frayed faster than it could be sewn, the ventilator on the sugar house that turned into a dormer, the three-toned moose, and Paul Bunyan's cauliflower ear that

38 (above). Flowers of the Bible; Fir block.

39 (below). Flowers of the Bible; Melon block.

had to be blanket-stitched to the sky. There were special satisfactions to be shared, also, in materials that had been found for special effects: a curve of white lace for a gliding gull, a rough white seersucker for the Portland Headlight, and pieces of old Battenburg trim in the shape of pine trees where pine trees were required.

Dorothy Sanborn, Bridgton, Maine

Designing the Patchwork Quilt

A patchworker's main concern is to combine modern or traditional blocks to make a colorful, geometric, fabric jigsaw puzzle. The design need not be original. A fresh interpretation of an antique pattern can result in a masterpiece. Old patchwork quilts often have a charming, spontaneous, random look that is difficult to duplicate with today's fabrics. Careful planning will guarantee successful patchwork as well as appliqué quilts.

REINTERPRETING TRADITIONAL PIECED PATTERNS

Many dull quilts have been made from very complex patchwork patterns. Your ability to unflinchingly piece a Mariner's Compass or a Carpenter's Wheel deserves sincere applause, but it does not guarantee that you will produce a beautiful quilt. It is not the pattern itself, but rather your interpretation of that pattern that brings a quilt to life. Gepetto interpreted a pile of wood, and he called it Pinocchio. The same pile of wood could have been Howdy Doody. Or it could just as easily have been a thousand toothpicks. It is our belief that simplicity does not mean you have to wind up with the toothpicks;

you can choose simple patterns and still produce an arrestingly beautiful quilt.

Leslie Carabas, a Berkeley, California, quilter, used the Star of the Sea design (figure 40) to piece five different wallhangings, each made from six Star of the Sea blocks, set solid. Figures 41 through 45 graphically illustrate how important interpretation can be. These wallhangings are all the same pattern, yet each one looks very different from the others because of Leslie's ingenious use of color and patterned fabrics.

DESIGNING WITH FABRIC GRAPHS

Patchwork quilts are easier for most people to envision than are appliqué quilts. A sketch of the quilt, drawn on graph paper and colored with marking pens, will help a group to imagine what the finished quilt will look like. But the most accurate way to see a finished quilt before it is sewn is to make a fabric graph, a scale model of the quilt, made on graph paper and using the actual quilt fabric. One of our authors, Judy Robbins, who has written step-by-step directions for fabric graphs in her book *Not Just Another Quilt*, has some suggestions for this: First, draw your block pattern to

41–45. Star of the Sea; variations A, B, C, D, and E.

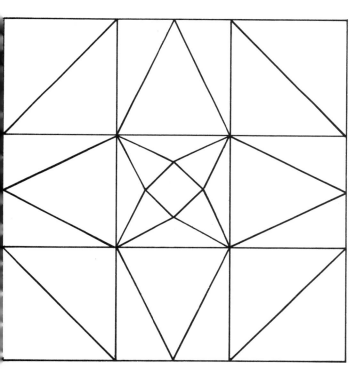

40. The Star of the Sea block.

measure approximately two inches on graph paper. From this small drawing, draft tiny templates. Holding each template under your thumb against several layers of fabric, cut small patches. Glue these into place on your graph paper drawing, using glue stick. Fabric graphs create very accurate renderings of the quilt, enabling a group to make informed color and design decisions.

ESTIMATING THE TIME AND DIFFICULTY OF PIECED PATTERNS

The simplest way to estimate how long it will take to make a patchwork block is to count the number of pieces. Each seam on each piece will have to be marked, cut, pinned, sewn, and pressed. It stands to reason that a block with nine pieces will be finished more quickly than will a block with 27 pieces. And 16-inch blocks will produce a quilt top faster than will 12-inch blocks. But time is much more of a concern for the individual quilter than it is for a group. Many of us would welcome the chance to piece one Mariner's Compass, but few of us have the time or inclination to piece 46 of these difficult blocks. Cooperative quilting allows us the freedom to participate in projects that would be impractical to undertake alone.

Judging the difficulty of patterns is a more personal matter. Beginning piecers would do well to avoid curved seams, long bias-y triangles, geometric figures with many points coming together in the center, and diamond shapes. Each of these involves sewing techniques that, though easily learned, are nevertheless apt to cause difficulties for those new to piecing. But exceptions prove the rule, and we know a number of people who have made masterful quilts, never realizing that the patterns they had selected would have intimidated more experienced quilters. The Tea Box block, also known as Tumbling block or Baby block, is made from infuriatingly stretchy diamonds. Women from the Storrs, Connecticut, Congregational Church hand pieced them without a hitch (see C-13 in color section).

We had seen a Tea Box Quilt in a magazine, with names of A. Lincoln and others done in silks. We made our quilt in three months—crazy timing, but it was our first one, and we didn't realize what we were attempting to do. Our sewers pieced the tea boxes with very little trouble. Afterwards, people told us we had tackled a hard design.

Janet Aronson, Coventry, Connecticut

Additional Design Concerns

In addition to the design concerns specific to patchwork and appliqué, there are some common challenges. These include color, sets, sashes, and borders. Let's take a look at each of these topics and see how we can deal creatively with these decisions.

PLANNING COLORS

Creative use of color is the most important gift you can give your quilt. Cooperative quilts, which presumably do not have to match your curtains, present unlimited possibilities for the free use of color. Because so many of us are unsure of ourselves, however, when it comes time to decide for the group, inhibitions suddenly appear. We choose "safe" colors—off-whites, blues, browns, and neutrals. Neutral colors are the lowest common denominator. They fit in many circumstances, and nobody objects to them, but it is also easy to yawn and fall asleep in their presence. There really is no reason to choose dull colors when each of us has the ability to be more adventurous.

Imagine, for a moment, that you have a good friend, a next-door neighbor, who is a talented artist, well known for her exquisite color sense. Not a quiltmaker herself, she loves to help you choose colors for your quilting projects. She raids your fabric hoard, cutting up three-inch samples that she takes home and combines into ingenious color palettes that she mounts on pieces of heavy white paper for you to look at. All you have to do is pick your favorites. Choosing is easy because the colors have already been artfully coordinated, you have a limited number of palettes to view, and nothing is left to the imagination. The choices are clearly visible.

For several years, Judy's students have been introduced to just such a "friend" in the form of picture magazines, the kind whose reputation demands that each photograph be a masterpiece of color and composition—*Smithsonian*, *National Geographic*, *Audubon*, *Arizona Highways*, and others like them that you have saved because they are too beautiful to throw away. To convert color photos to fabric palettes for your quilts, try this exercise: tear out any color pictures that appeal to you. Do not worry about the size or the subject matter. An ideal color scheme may appear in a whiskey ad or in magnified biology slides. Once you have found an appealing photographic color scheme, you are halfway there. Now, choose one picture and sit down with a basket of small fabric samples. These may be three-inch squares cut from your own collection, or smaller samples from mail-order fabric dealers. Build a palette by laying fabric samples down right on top of the photograph, selecting those that approximate the colors in your picture. Print fabrics will give you texture where it is necessary. Once you have put together a number of fabrics that look good with the photo, remove the picture and lay your fabrics against white paper. Do you still like what you see? Just as you would correct seasonings in a soup, take this time to make any necessary color adjustments. Try the exercise alone, then try it with your group. Working out these palettes will develop your intuitive understanding of color, in addition to breaking up habitual color choices.

Palette building as a group allows many people to have input into what is usually a one- or two-person decision—picking out your quilt's color scheme. Everyone can bring in photos and fabric samples. You can either go through the pictures and choose one that you all like, working together to build one palette, or you can work separately with different photos, each creating your own palette to be offered at the end of the meeting as one possible choice. When one color scheme has been agreed upon, overlap the chosen fabric samples and sew or glue them to a card. The fabric buyers can then take this card with the fabric palette to the quilt shop; it will make shopping much easier because the group will have already narrowed down the range of acceptable fabrics. The buyers will be able to look through several hundred bolts and still maintain their focus. Because of limited selection and out-of-print fabrics, they will probably have to

make some substitutions to the original palette, but if these are kept in the same color and scale, they will not alter the integrity of the original plan.

PLANNING SETS

The way the blocks are arranged on the quilt top is called the *set*. A simple quilt can be made to look more intriguing by an unusual set. A simple pieced block, like that in the Propeller Quilt shown in the pattern section (see figure 118) can appear more complex by setting the blocks solid and running the rows of blocks diagonally across the quilt. This set encourages interesting secondary patterns to emerge, doubling the effect of many simple patterns.

46. Barely Enough.

Sometimes pieced quilt blocks can be rotated, upended, or otherwise placed in novel sets. This is the case with Barely Enough (figure 46), a contemporary wallhanging designed by Jan Inouye and Ann Rhode as one of three raffle quilts for the East Bay Heritage Quilters in the San Francisco Bay area.

Perhaps you may choose to design your quilt with alternating blocks. Traditionally, the blocks are laid out pieced, plain, pieced, plain, and so on across the surface of the quilt like the Snail Trail Quilt shown in the pattern section (see figure 79). Often the plain blocks are embellished later with fancy quilting. This is a viable way to set a pieced quilt,

47 and 48. Footlights at Wolftrap; block 1 above and block 2 below (copyright Judy Spahn, 1983).

and if a group especially likes quilting together, it may be a good choice for them.

Judy Spahn alternated two pieced blocks in her "Footlights at Wolf Trap" (see C-23 in color section), a quilt she designed for Quilters Unlimited of Northern Virginia to raffle for the benefit of the Wolf Trap Park for the Performing Arts. Pictured in figures 47 and 48 are the two blocks. Can you find them in a repeating, alternating pattern in the quilt? (Hint: The quilt is surrounded with a border of half-blocks.)

Daisy Chain (see C-21 in color section) is also made up of two alternating blocks. The more complex of the two is Judy Martin's own update of Variable Star. The second, or filler, block is very simple, pieced only in the corners, and yet when these blocks are set together, the quilt really sings with movement. The simple alternate block creates fascinating curves in the design. You would not expect so dramatic a transformation from such a simple design.

The quilt Rosemary Corbin of Point Richmond, California, coordinated to finance her friend's school board campaign, also uses alternating blocks in a novel way. The quilt (see figure 19) combines patchwork and appliqué in Schoolhouse blocks alternating with school scenes, emphasizing the theme of this raffle quilt.

We have also seen a few pictorial quilts that alternate appliquéd blocks with plain blocks. This is not quite as easy to do effectively. It is critical that the color of the plain block be very closely coordinated to the appliquéd blocks, so that the checkerboard effect is minimized. Sometimes these quilts look as if something were missing, as though only half the proper number of appliqué blocks had been available. Perhaps this is a matter of taste, but we prefer pictorial quilts that have busy, lively surfaces. Empty spaces work well only when they are planned to complement the pieced or appliquéd areas.

Patchwork blocks will be set together in a predetermined way, so you will not have to spend time later figuring out where each block should go. By contrast, many pictorial quilts feature a different scene on each block, and you will not be able to determine final block placement until you see the finished blocks. The temptation will be to lay these finished blocks out on the floor, but you will get a much better view if you can pin the blocks to a wall. Pin up the sashing too, if you are planning to use it. Stand back to see how the blocks look from a distance. We all tend to become involved with

49. Choosing the layout for the Cambridge Women's Quilt.

work, sashes can deliberately discourage secondary patterns by keeping each block a distinct unit (for example, C-19 in color section). Sashing eliminates the need for exact matching of pieced blocks, and this can be a great advantage if the finished blocks are likely to vary slightly in size.

Plain sashes can fulfill their framing function quite artfully. Both the Marine Mammal and the Eureka, California, commemorative quilt, Origins (see C-16 and C-22 in color section) use double sashing to set off each block. The first sash is narrow, and the second band is wider. This has the same effect as double matting on a painting or print.

We have included one antique quilt, Rosetta Burr's Friendship Quilt (figure 97 in the pattern section). It boasts a rather outrageous plaid sashing, and this unexpected fabric works well to draw the viewer's eye to the sawtooth effect of the triangles along its length. When used as part of the patchwork, unusual fabrics are often cut too small to show themselves to advantage, but borders and sashing can showcase some of your favorite nonconformist fabrics.

Pieced sashes themselves can also become areas of particular interest in your quilt. These may be simple pieced strips like the "road" sashing in Beyer Beware (C-6 in color section) or, as Betty Boyink demonstrates in her Religious Symbols (see figure 20), they may be even more elaborate than the quilt blocks. Other quilts, like the Ohio Star Quilt in the pattern section (see figure 110), feature sashes pieced only at the corners of the blocks. The three-dimensional illusion sashing in the appliquéd Claremont (California) Quilt (figure 50) can also be used with pieced patterns.

The Green Acres Bird Quilt (see figure 1) demonstrates yet another novel use of sashing. The narrow black sash, made of grosgrain ribbon, gives viewers the feeling that they are seeing the appliquéd scene through a large window.

Interesting borders can give a quilt another focal point. In the Boone Bicentennial Sampler (see figure 3) barber-pole stripes create a broad, bold edge for a busy quilt. The simple schoolyard scene in the Rainbow Fantasy Quilt (see figure 9) has a wide rainbow-striped border. Different fantasy scenes—a dragon, a castle, a unicorn—are set into the stripes. Borders can be narrow or wide, simple or ornate, subtle or bold, depending on what will best complement the quilt. Varying the sets, sashes, and borders can transform simple patterns into quilts with distinctive character and personality.

the pictures on appliqué blocks, and the tunnel vision this creates impairs our ability to see the quilt as a whole. Take instant-developing pictures of the various block arrangements to remind you what the different sets look like.

PLANNING SASHES AND BORDERS

We usually think of sashing as a series of frames, setting each block apart from the others. In patch-

50. Claremont Quilt.

General Appliqué Directions

An old aphorism advises, "It takes a fine needle to sew a fine seam." If the needles in your pincushion look like carpentry nails, there's not much chance of achieving that "fine seam." So, your first step is to supply yourself with good tools. Number 8 sharps are the traditional favorite for hand sewing, but quilting needles (size 8, 9, or 10) will work just as well. Equipment should also include a well-fitting thimble, small sharp scissors, and a variety of fabrics. For making templates, you will need an assortment of pencils, paper, lightweight cardboard or pattern plastic, and scissors for cutting paper.

MAKING PATTERNS

Using a pencil, draw your scene full size. If the scene is very large, you may have to use rolls of brown paper taped together. When you have a sketch that you like, go over the pencil lines with a felt-tip marker. This is your master copy, the source for your patterns.

Now make the patterns. Using tracing paper or cheap typing paper, outline each shape and cut it out. Mark the right side of each template with a word or two that identifies it. Later, you will have several funny little paper shapes, and you will be glad you labeled "car bumper" or "upper left cloud" on the templates. If the templates are to be used only once, the paper template may suffice; otherwise, glue the paper template to lightweight cardboard.

The master drawing will help determine which pieces to sew down first. Begin with the larger background pieces, and sew the smaller foreground pieces later. You may find that some of the pieces appear to overlap. You can eliminate some unnecessary sewing by extending the "background" pattern piece under the "foreground" pattern piece. In figure 51, triangle A overlaps triangle B. The extended template for triangle B is shown in figure 52. Mark the B template at the points where A overlaps so that you will clearly see where to position A. It is not necessary to sew down the corner of B that extends under A.

(When sewing appliqués, it is easiest to secure and sew one piece at a time rather than to assemble the whole scene and try to sew it all down at once. In the preceding example, triangle B would be secured and sewn down first; then triangle A would be attached.)

CUTTING THE FABRICS

When all the templates have been made, lay them out, puzzle fashion, to form your scene. This is a good way to check the accuracy of the templates before you cut your fabrics.

To cut the fabric, lay the template on the *right* side of the fabric and trace the template with a pencil or water-erasable marker. Cut approximately ¼ inch outward from the traced lines to allow the raw edges to be turned under.

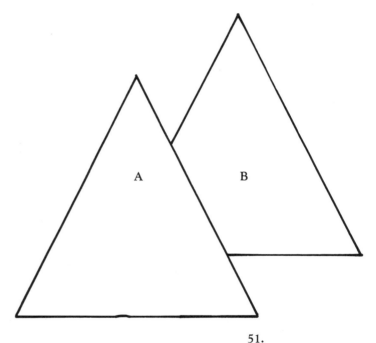

51.

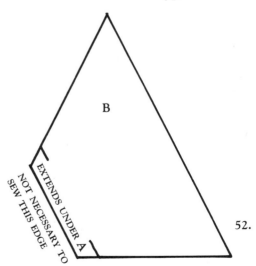

52.

PREPARING THE APPLIQUÉS

To prepare the appliqué for stitching, the raw edges must be turned under. There are three ways to do this.

BASTING

Although basting the raw edges to the wrong side of the appliqué is time consuming, it makes the actual appliquéing go much more quickly and probably equalizes the time in the long run. Roll the raw edge between thumb and forefinger to the wrong side. The pencil line marks the crease. Sew with two or three stitches per inch (figure 53), and use a contrasting-color thread so the basting stitches can be seen clearly for easy removal later. But be careful. We have had the experience of basting white appliqués with red thread, only to find that the red left a series of dots where the dye had rubbed off in the needle holes. Now we always baste with pastel-colored thread. To facilitate removal of the basting, keep the knots on the right side of the appliqué and do not knot the last stitch.

IRONING

Seam allowances can also be ironed to the wrong side over a lightweight cardboard template (figure 54). This works particularly well with cotton fabrics. If the fabric does not want to lay flat, dampen it slightly before ironing or try steam ironing.

NEEDLE TUCKING

The third method is to turn the raw edges in and appliqué at the same time (figure 55). Pin or baste the appliqué in place and tuck the raw edge under with the point of the needle, just ahead of the stitching.

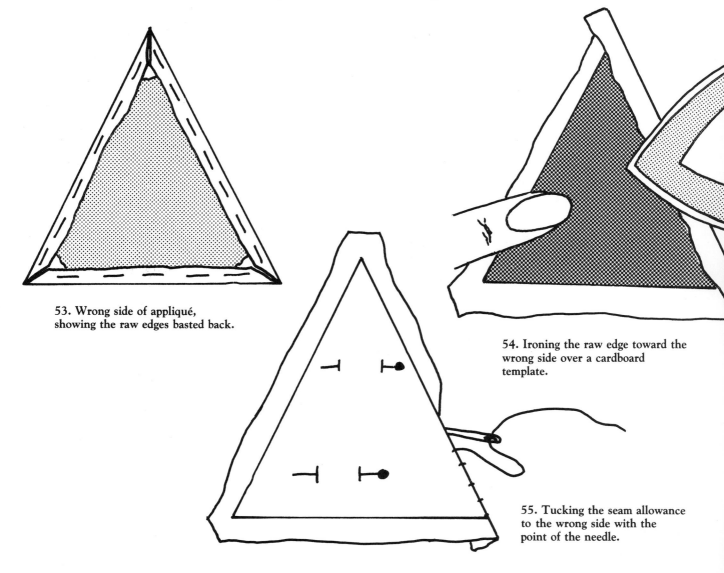

53. Wrong side of appliqué, showing the raw edges basted back.

54. Ironing the raw edge toward the wrong side over a cardboard template.

55. Tucking the seam allowance to the wrong side with the point of the needle.

STITCHING

Appliqués should be stitched in order, from the background pieces to the foreground pieces. They can be held to the ground fabric with pins, but the pin heads provide obstacles that catch and tangle the thread. An alternative to pinning is basting the appliqué to the ground with thread. Another alternative is spot-gluing the appliqués in place with glue stick. Many traditionalists are shocked at such an unorthodox method, but it actually has historical precedent. Traditionally, many fine, sheer Swiss appliqués were held in place with wheat paste during stitching. Later the entire piece was washed, dissolving the flour-and-water paste. Glue stick is washable, but we have not found it to be obtrusive even when it is not washed out.

When stitching the appliqués to the background, use thread matched to the appliqué (not to the background), and keep your knots on the wrong side. Figures 56 through 62 show five popular appliqué stitches. The terms "appliqué stitch" and "blind stitch" are often used interchangeably to refer to any stitch that is almost invisible, but there are actually two different stitches that will produce this effect.

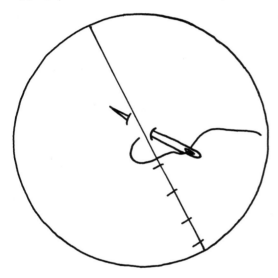

56. Magnified view of the **appliqué stitch;** keep stitches about ⅛ inch apart.

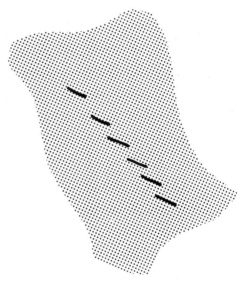

57. This is how your **appliqué stitch** will look from the wrong side.

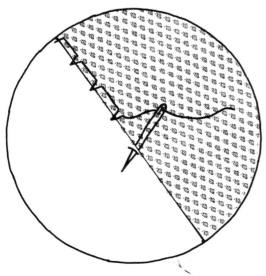

58. To do the **blind stitch,** move the needle ahead invisibly in the fold of the appliqué. Bring the needle out of the fold to take tiny stitches in the background fabric every ⅛ inch.

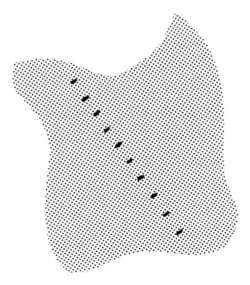

59. This is how your **blind stitch** will look on the wrong side.

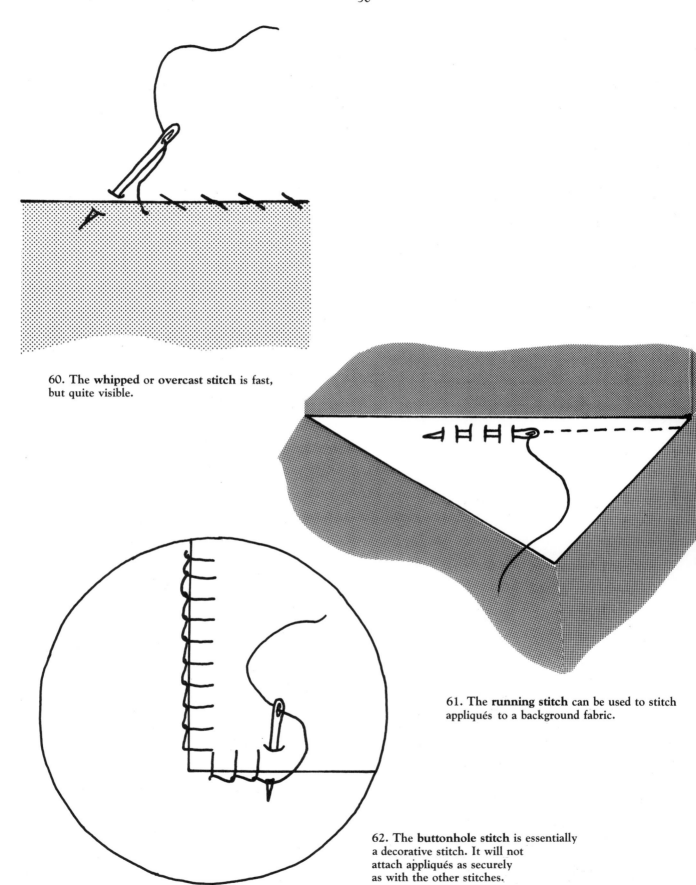

60. The **whipped** or **overcast stitch** is fast, but quite visible.

61. The **running stitch** can be used to stitch appliqués to a background fabric.

62. The **buttonhole stitch** is essentially a decorative stitch. It will not attach appliqués as securely as with the other stitches.

TECHNIQUES

Figures 63 through 74 show six common appliqué situations and suggestions for sewing. We have seen appliqués embellished with ribbons, buttons, feathers, shells, and shisha mirrors. All manner of things can be added to your appliqués, especially if your quilt is a wall hanging and will not receive the normal wear and tear. But we caution you to temper inspiration with appropriate common sense, so that these "extras" will be in the spirit of the rest of the quilt.

To finish the appliqué quilt, see "Putting the Quilt Together" in the following section.

63. Clip an **inside curve** almost to the seam line. Make as few clips as possible, because they weaken the appliqué. Sew the clipped areas with closer-than-usual appliqué stitches.

64. Opinions differ on the best way to sew an **outside curve.** Some quilters clip the curve as shown above. Others think that the clips make the curve harder to sew, and so refrain from clipping. They distribute the extra fabric in the outside curve with their fingers or the point of their needle.

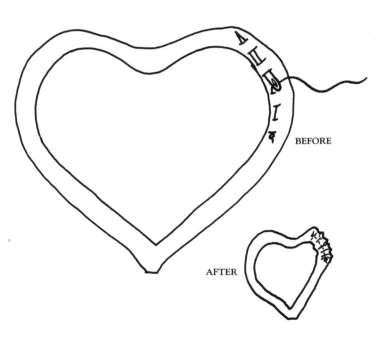

BEFORE

AFTER

65. Another way to deal with an outside curve is to run a gathering thread just outside the pencil line. When drawn up, the gathering thread distributes the extra fabric in the curve, and the outside curve turns back smoothly.

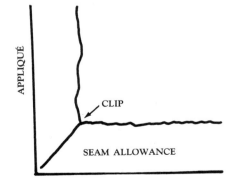

APPLIQUÉ

CLIP

SEAM ALLOWANCE

66. Clip an inside corner almost to the seam line.

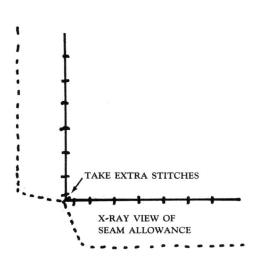

TAKE EXTRA STITCHES

X-RAY VIEW OF
SEAM ALLOWANCE

67. Turn back the seam allowance.
Sew an extra stitch or two in the
corner to reinforce.

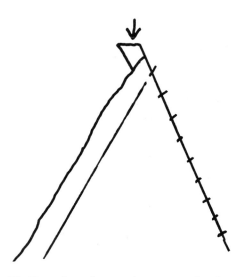

70. To make a sharp **point**, turn under the
seam allowance and sew to the point.
Trim the overhang to reduce bulk.

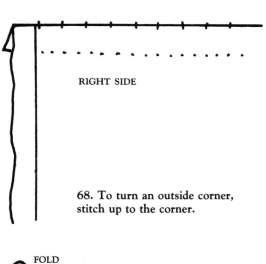

RIGHT SIDE

68. To turn an outside corner,
stitch up to the corner.

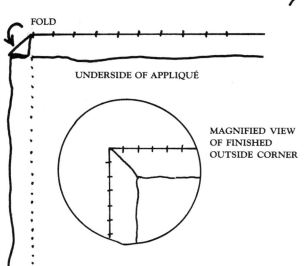

FOLD

UNDERSIDE OF APPLIQUÉ

MAGNIFIED VIEW
OF FINISHED
OUTSIDE CORNER

69. Miter by folding the seam allowance
to the back at an angle. Fold the remaining
seam allowance to the back along
the seam line.

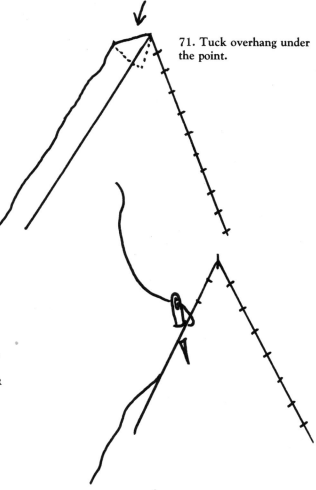

71. Tuck overhang under
the point.

72. Turn back the remaining seam allowance and stitch.
If the point is part of a very sharp angle, trim the
seam allowance in the point area to a scant ⅛ inch.

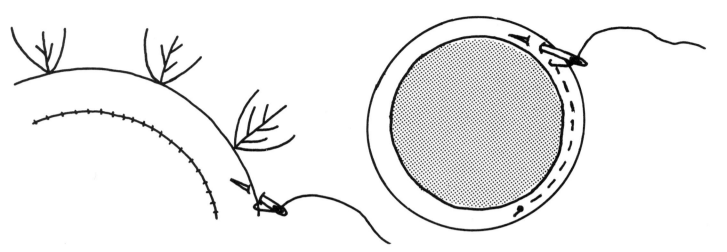

73. **Bias tape,** either purchased or homemade, is often used for stems and other curved lines. Always sew the shorter side first; then when you sew the longer side, it will ease to fit.

74. For **circles,** first press the seam allowances back over a lightweight cardboard template. Then gather the seam allowance by drawing a gathering thread to fit. Before the gathering thread is secured, remove the cardboard.

General Patchwork Directions

For patchwork, you will need pattern plastic or lightweight cardboard, an assortment of well-sharpened pencils, and two pairs of scissors, one for cutting paper and the other for cutting fabric. A clear plastic ruler imprinted with a grid of ⅛-inch squares is helpful for adding seam allowances. And, of course, you will need your selection of fabrics.

PATTERN DRAFTING

Most quilt patterns (including the ones in this book) do not include seam allowances. To make templates from full-size patterns, *carefully* follow these steps:
1. Trace each pattern piece onto tracing paper.
2. Using glue stick, affix the tracing paper to pattern plastic, cardboard, or sandpaper.
3. Add exact ¼-inch seams.
4. Cut out the template and label it with the name of the quilt pattern as well as the letter or number of its piece (e.g., Snail Trail A, as shown in figure 75).

This produces a template that includes the seam allowances. When this template is traced onto the wrong side of the fabric, the pencil marks the *cutting* line. Many hand piecers prefer a template without the seams because this allows them to mark the ac-

tual *sewing* line. If this is your preference, skip step 3 (above). *After the templates are made, make a sample block out of scrap fabric to test the accuracy of your templates.* This will also serve as a sample for the other blocks.

CUTTING THE FABRIC

If necessary, iron prewashed fabric so that you have a smooth surface for tracing. To make the most economical use of fabric, cut border strips and sashing first; then cut larger pieces before the smaller ones. As a general rule, one or more straight sides of the template should be on the straight grain of the fabric. Place the template face down on the wrong side of the fabric, and trace with a sharp pencil. If a block contains reversed patterns, turn the template face up. Mark templates for reversed patterns "R."

Templates that are drafted with seam allowance included can be traced interlocking (figure 76). For templates that do not include the seam allowance, tracings must be spaced at least ½ inch apart to allow for seams. The cutting line is then gauged "by eye" at approximately the midpoint of the space between the two tracings (figure 77).

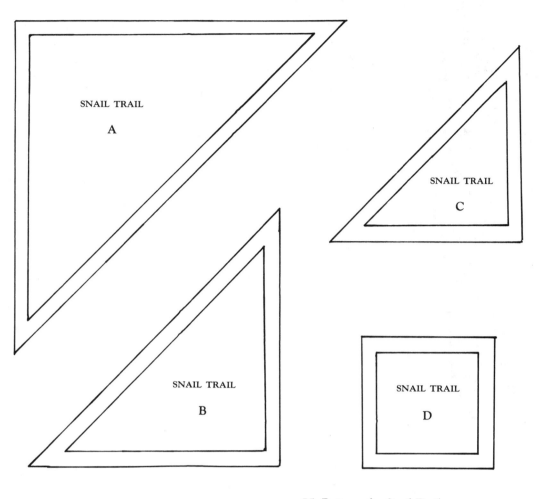

**75. Patterns for Snail Trail;
these include seam allowances.**

HAND SEWING

Right sides together, line up two patches, matching the pencilled seam lines, and pin to hold the line in place. With a #7 or #8 needle and a single thread knotted at the end, use the running stitch to sew along the pencil line from beginning to end, finishing with a secure knot (figure 78).

MACHINE SEWING

When sewing by machine, use a template that includes the seam allowance. Align the cut edges of two patches. Sew from edge to edge, keeping a ¼-inch seam. Most machines have a scored throat plate that will indicate the ¼-inch measurement. Other machines feature a wide presser-foot that can be used to guide your ¼-inch seam. If your machine has neither, place a piece of masking tape on the throat plate ¼ inch away from the needle and use this as a guide.

PRESSING AND ASSEMBLY

Seams are not pressed open in quiltmaking; they are pressed toward one side. Press each finished block flat before joining it to another block. The easiest way to assemble a quilt is to join the blocks in horizontal rows. Then seam the rows together to form the quilt top.

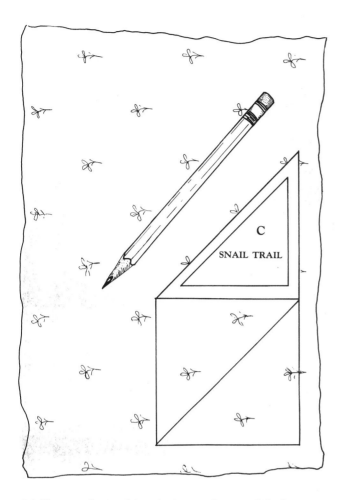

76. Patterns for machine piecing can be traced flush; use the wrong side of the fabric.

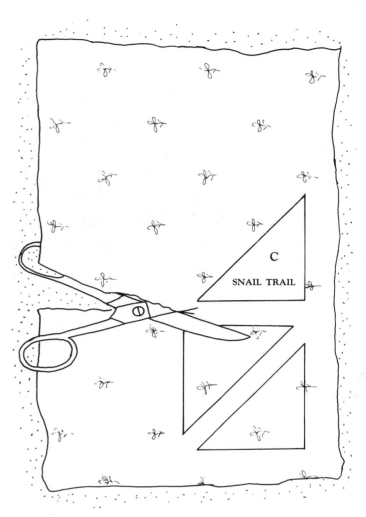

77. Patterns spaced for hand sewing, ½ inch apart; traced line is the sewing line. The cutting line is the "eyeball estimate," midway between the templates, approximately ¼ inch from each template.

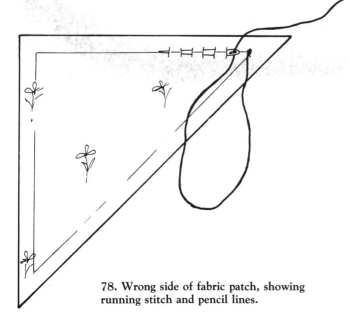

78. Wrong side of fabric patch, showing running stitch and pencil lines.

MARKING FOR QUILTING

Sometimes a quilt will be quilted along the outlines of the patchwork design, eliminating the need for marking. But fancy quilting designs will need to be marked on the quilt top. Trace the quilting design onto paper, using a black felt-tip marker. Lay the quilt top over the marked paper and trace lightly, directly on the right side of the quilt top with a hard pencil. If fabrics are opaque, a light box may be useful. If you wish, you can make a perforated stencil by tracing the design onto lightweight cardboard, and then going over the tracing with an un-threaded sewing machine set to about five or six stitches per inch. Center the template on the quilt and pounce by rubbing powder through the holes (cinnamon for light-colored fabrics and talc or cornstarch for darks). The pounced design rubs off quickly, so trace it again with pencil.

PUTTING THE QUILT TOGETHER

After the quilt top is finished and marked, you will be ready to assemble the quilt "sandwich:" the backing, a layer of batting, and, finally, the pieced or appliquéd quilt top.

MAKING THE BACKING

We recommend printed fabric as a backing for co-operative quilts. The print helps disguise uneven stitching and creates an attractive complement to the pieced top. Quilt backings should be made at least two to three inches larger on each side than the quilt top. Usually two or three lengths of fabric must be seamed together to form a backing large enough for such a quilt. To avoid puckers, cut away the selvedge edge from the backing material. Sew with ¼-inch seams.

LAYERING AND BASTING

Lay down the backing on a large, flat surface, seam side up. Spread the batting carefully over this, being sure both layers stay smooth and wrinkle free. Complete the quilt sandwich by laying on the quilt top, right side up. Smooth out any wrinkles and check that any seams on the top are parallel to seams on the backing. Pin the three layers together as necessary to hold them steady while you baste.

Baste the layers together using four- to six-inch stitches and a long needle. First baste an **X** on the quilt, starting in the center and working out to the corners. Then baste in rows four to six inches apart. If the quilt is to be quilted in a large floor frame, basting can be rather sparse, but if the quilt is to be quilted in a hoop and handled by many people, then generous basting is recommended.

TYING AND QUILTING

Quilts can be tied with soft yarn (threads with a hard finish like embroidery floss are abrasive and create holes in the fabric). Thread the yarn double through a sharp, large-eyed needle. Pull the yarn through all three layers of the quilt at the corners of the blocks and at any other logical intersections. Cut the yarn tails to about three inches and tie in a square knot. Trim the yarn tails if desired.

We prefer quilts that are hand quilted, as opposed to tied; tying has a utilitarian look to us. Hand quilting adds a dimensional quality and provides lots of opportunity to work with your group around the frame. If you are creating a fundraiser, hand quilting will increase your earnings considerably.

In order to hand quilt, put the quilt into a hoop or frame and quilt through all three layers with a close running stitch. All knots should be concealed by pulling them through into the batting. Some quilters avoid knots by beginning and ending with back stitching.

BINDING AND FINISHING

When the quilting is finished, trim the batt and backing so they are even with the quilt top. Place a 1 ¾-inch binding strip on one edge of the quilt top, right sides together. Sew through all the layers with a ¼-inch seam. Repeat for the other three sides. Fold the binding to the back, tucking under ¼ inch and blindstitching it over the previous seam. Sew your name and date on the back of the quilt or attach a label.

Six Patchwork Patterns

The patterns featured here are all traditional American quilts. They are tried-and-true proven favorites across the country. None of these quilts is so difficult that it will inhibit a newly formed group of quilters.

Of course, any pattern from any source may be used with our guide to cooperative quiltmaking (Chapter 3), but any one of these patterns will get your group off to a successful beginning.

SNAIL TRAIL QUILT

The advantage of this pattern in a cooperative quilt is that pieced blocks are set with plain blocks in between. This means that there is no need for matching—a great advantage when there are several sewers of different skill levels. The quilt shown in figure 79 is made with two fabrics. Although sharply contrasting fabrics will give this quilt a very bold look, the makers of this quilt opted for more subtle colors, since the scale of the quilt is quite bold already.

79. Snail Trail.

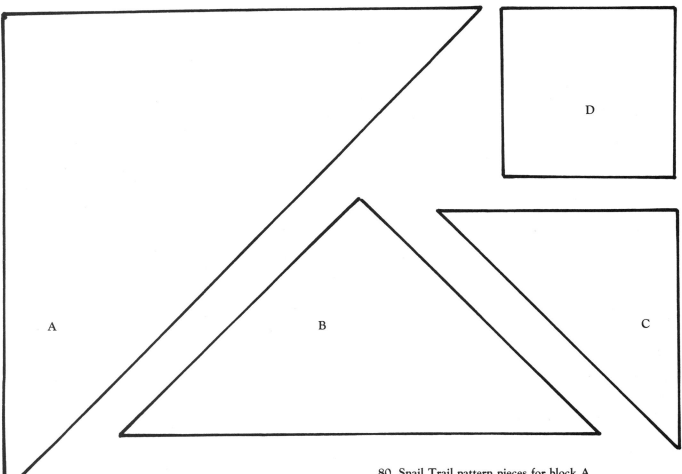

80. Snail Trail pattern pieces for block A (block B is a solid 10-inch square for which no pattern is given).

Quilt size: 84″ x 104″
Block size: 10″ (set 7 x 9)
Border sizes (without seam allowances):
  print border 2″
  solid border 1″
  print border 4″
Yardage (44″ fabric):
  print 4 yds.
  solid 4 yds.
  backing 6½ yds.
  batting 86″ x 106″
Quilt requires: 32 A blocks; 31 B blocks.
Each A block requires:
  print 2A, 2B, 2C, 2D;
  solid 2A, 2B, 2C, 2D.
B blocks, 10″ x 10″ (without seam allowances):
  print 16;
  solid 15.
Techniques: machine or hand piecing; hand quilting.
Degree of difficulty: very easy.

ASSEMBLY

1. Keep ¼-inch seams throughout. Piece the A blocks first. Sew a print D-square piece to a solid D-square piece. Repeat (figure 81). Sew the two DD units together as shown in figure 82. Sew the two solid C-triangle pieces to the resulting unit (figure 83). Repeat with two print C triangles (figure 84). Sew the two solid B triangles and then the two print B triangles to the existing unit (figure 85). In the same manner, sew the A triangles to this BCD unit (figure 86). Press well. Repeat to make 32 blocks.

2. Cut the B blocks, and lay them out alternately with the A blocks.

3. Assemble the quilt in horizontal rows, referring to the photo for block placement. Sew the horizontal rows together to form the top of the quilt. Then seam the borders to the large unit. Press.

4. Mark the quilting design on the finished quilt top with a hard lead pencil or water-erasable marker. Use a plastic coffee-can lid or similar round object for your quilting template. Center the template on a plain square. Mark or notch the template at the four corners of the square (figure 87). From these notches, extend curved lines that arc into the center squares of the surrounding blocks (figure 88). If you feel a template is necessary for this arc, you can make one out of pattern plastic. Mark the entire quilt top.

5. Prepare the backing fabric by sewing it to allow about 4 inches extra on each side. Layer and baste the quilt.

6. Put the quilt into a frame and hand quilt.

7. Bind the edges and finish with a personalized label on the back.

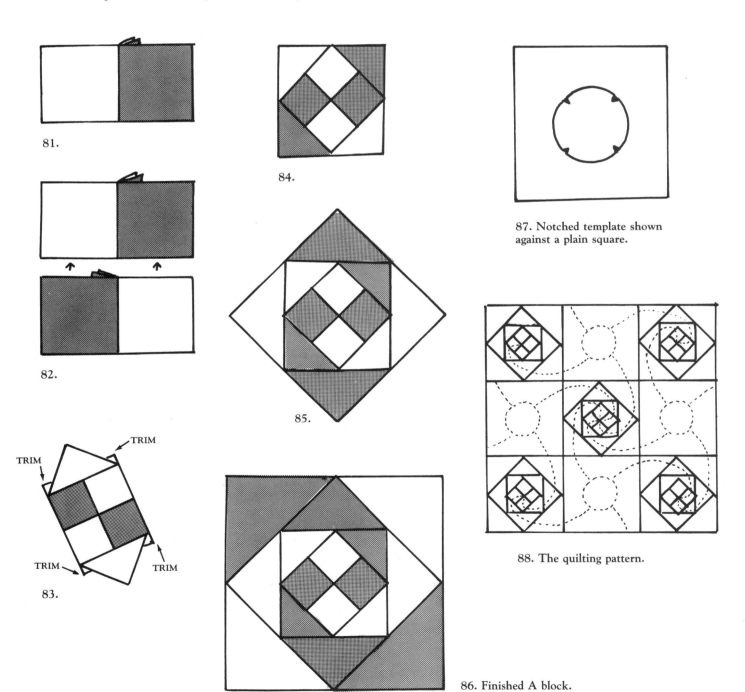

81.

82.

83.

84.

85.

86. Finished A block.

87. Notched template shown against a plain square.

88. The quilting pattern.

89. Daisy Chain.

DAISY CHAIN QUILT

Daisy Chain is an intriguing pattern for a cooperative quilt because it combines two blocks, one a very simple "filler" block and the other a more complex star. This opens up many possibilities for the creative division of work. Beginners or very busy people could make the simple blocks, leaving the stars to more experienced sewers. Daisy Chain is full of movement and life, making it an appealing choice as a fundraiser. Scraps comprise almost half of the fabric for the top, so the quilt is as inexpensive as it is beautiful. Designed by Judy Martin for *Quilter's Newsletter* and *Quiltmaker* magazines, it can be seen in all its glory as C-21 in the color section.

ASSEMBLY

1. For the A block: Sew a dark A piece to each of the four long sides of a muslin B piece. Repeat to make 49 A blocks (figure 91).
2. For the B block: Sew a light A to a dark A to form a square Unit 1 (figure 92). Repeat three times.
3. Sew a pink C to one side of muslin D and a pink Cr to the other side of D to form a square Unit 2 (figure 93). Repeat three times.
4. See figure 94: Sew a Unit 2 between two Unit 1's. Repeat. Sew the remaining Unit 2 squares to opposite sides of a muslin E. Sew the three segments together as shown to complete the B block. Repeat to make 50 B blocks (figure 95).

Quilt size: 80″ x 95″
Block size: 7½″ (set 9 x 11)
Border sizes (without seam allowances):
   muslin border 1¼″
   pieced border 2½″
   pink border 2½″
Yardage (44″ fabric):
   muslin 4¼ yds.
   pink 3 yds.
   light scraps 1½ yds.
   dark scraps 2¼ yds.
   backing 5½ yds.
   batting 82″ x 97″
Quilt requires: 49 A blocks; 50 B blocks.
Each A block requires:
   muslin 1B;
   dark scraps 4A.
Each B block requires:
   muslin 4D, 1E;
   pink 4C, 4Cr;
   light scraps 4A;
   dark scraps 4A.
Techniques: machine or hand piecing; hand quilting.
Degree of difficulty: intermediate.

90. Full-size patterns
for Daisy Chain.

ADD ¼″ SEAMS.

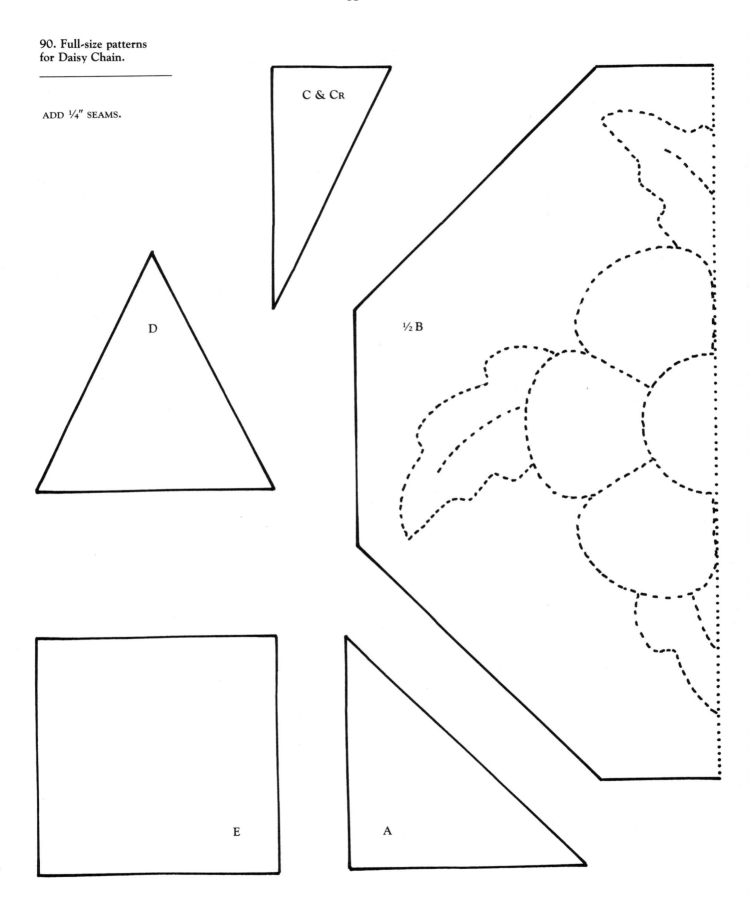

C & CR

D

½ B

E

A

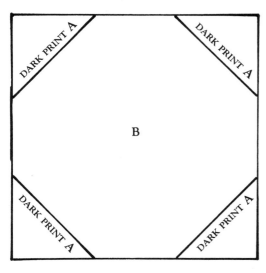

91. Finished A block.

92. Unit 1.

93. Unit 2.

96. Pieced border for sides, and for top and bottom (with corners sewn on).

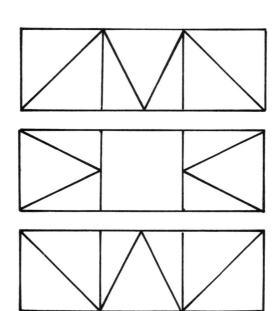

94. B block in progress.

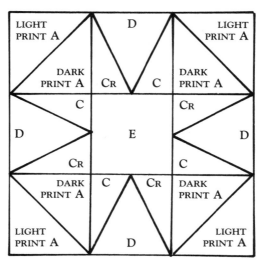

95. Finished B block.

SIDES

TOP AND BOTTOM

5. Sew 5 B blocks alternately with 4 A blocks to make a row of 9 blocks. Repeat to make six rows like this. Sew 5 A blocks alternately with 4 B blocks to make another row of 9 blocks. Repeat to make five of these rows. Sew the rows together, alternating those rows starting with an A block with those starting with a B block.

6. Add the muslin border. To make the second, pieced border, sew a dark A piece to a light A piece to form a square (a Unit 1). Repeat to make 128

squares. Sew squares in rows, as shown in figure 96, and add to the top, bottom, and sides of the quilt. Then add the third, pink border.

7. Mark quilting pattern in the octagons as shown on pattern piece B (see figure 90).

8. Seam backing together. Layer, baste, and place the quilt in a frame.

9. Quilt as marked. Outline-quilt the patches. Bind. Finish with a personalized label.

FRIENDSHIP QUILT

This old-time pattern has a plain muslin space in the center of each block, perfect for signatures or embroidery. The muslin triangles around the perimeter of each block combine visually to create a lively sawtooth effect all over the quilt. The pattern is simple enough for beginners, and the blocks can be outline quilted, eliminating the need for marking a separate design on the quilt top. Made with a variety of bright scraps, the traditional Friendship Quilt will be at home in any setting.

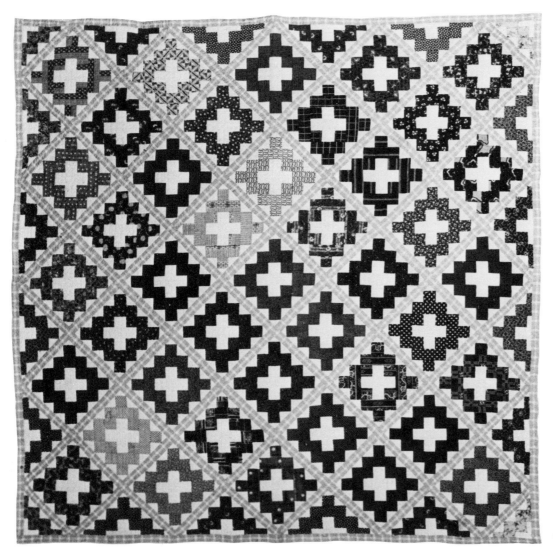

97. Friendship Quilt.

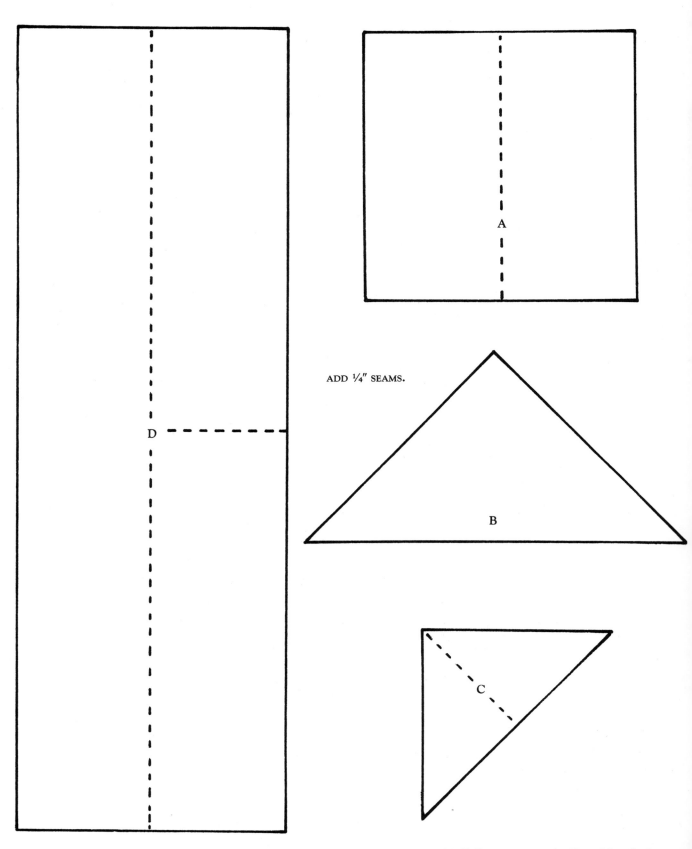

ADD ¼" SEAMS.

98. Full-size patterns for Friendship Quilt.

Quilt size: 106″ x 106″
Block size: 12″ (set diagonally)
Sashes and border (without seam allowances):
    2″
Yardage (44″ fabric):
                    muslin   5 yds.
                    scraps   4 yds.
    sashing and border   3 yds.
                    backing   9 yds. (A strip
                               approximately 3 yds. x
                               20″ will be left over to
                               use for piecing or
                               sashing, if desired.)
                    batting   108″ x 108″
Templates (make eight): A; half-A; B; C; half-
    C; D; half-D; quarter-D. Use dotted lines on
    the patterns in figure 98 to determine halves
    and quarters.
Quilt requires: 41 A blocks; 16 B blocks; and 4
    C blocks.
Each A block requires:
    muslin   2A, 8B, 4C, 1D;
    scraps   8A.
Each B block requires:
    muslin   1A, 4B, 1C, 2 half-C, 1 half-D;
    scraps   3A, 2 half-A.
Each C block requires:
    muslin   1 half-A, 2B, 2 half-C, 1 quarter-
              D;
    scraps   1A, 2 half-A.
Techniques: machine or hand piecing; hand
    quilting.
Degree of difficulty: easy.

ASSEMBLY

1. Assemble each A block by sewing the patches into diagonal rows (figure 99). Seam the rows together to form a finished A block (figure 100). Make 41 blocks.
2. Assemble all the B blocks, sewing the patches in diagonal rows as you did with the A blocks (figure 101). Make 16 of these.
3. Assemble the 4 C blocks (figures 102 and 103).
4. Sew a 12-inch sash to the right and left sides of each A block.
5. Following the photograph in figure 97, assemble the entire quilt top in diagonal rows, sewing strips of sashing in between the rows of blocks.
6. Add a border of the sashing material.
7. Seam the backing together. Layer, baste, and place the quilt in a frame.
8. Outline quilt. If you quilt ¼ inch away from the seams, you will avoid sewing through the seam allowance.
9. Trim and bind. Finish with a signature or label.

99 (left). **Assembling the A block pieces.**
100 (below). **Finished A block.**

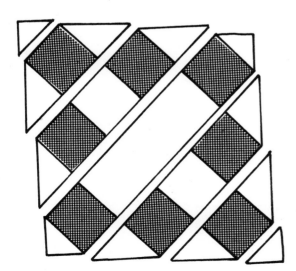

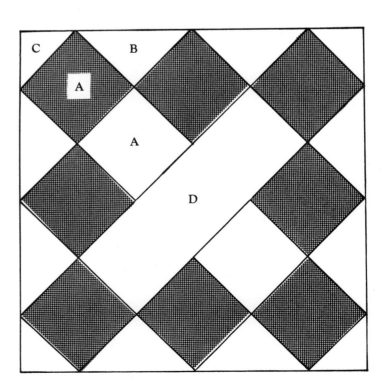

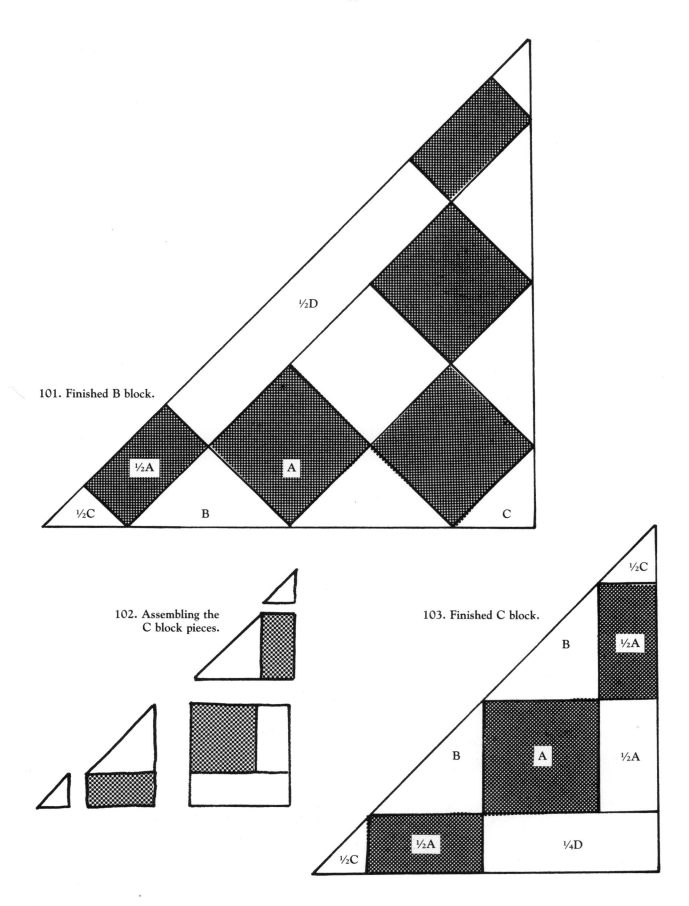

101. Finished B block.

102. Assembling the C block pieces.

103. Finished C block.

SHADOWS QUILT

Shadows, based on a traditional Amish design, is the perfect project for a group that loves hand quilting. The Amish, famous for their inventive use of vibrant solid-color fabrics and graphically simple patchwork patterns, lavish their quilts with intricate, exacting quilting. The quilting design for this Shadows Quilt comes from Philomena Wiechec, a talented interpreter of Celtic design. The over and under lines symbolize eternity in Philomena's adaptation of a design from the *Book of Kells*, an eighth-century illuminated manuscript. The quilting designs for the borders are Amish adaptations, slightly different from the border designs shown in the photograph. See C-12 in the color section for another look at this quilt, and be sure to consult the Resources section in the back of this book for more about Philomena Wiechec and her active quilting group, the Santa Clara Valley Quilt Association.

Quilt size: 68″ x 104″ (twin)
Block size: 12″ (set 4 x 7)
Border sizes   (without seam allowances):
      light border   3″
   medium border   1″
     dark border   6″
Yardage   (44″ fabric):
     dark   3 yds.
   medium   2 yds.
     light   1 yd.
   assorted solids to total 1 yd.
   backing   6 yds.
   batting   70″ x 106″
Quilt requires: 28 blocks.
Each block requires: 1A, 1B, 1C, 1D, 1E, 1F, 1G.
Techniques: machine or hand piecing; hand quilting.
Degree of difficulty: piecing, easy; quilting, intermediate.

ASSEMBLY

1. To piece the blocks, sew 1¼-inch strips cut from patterns B,C,D,E, and F together, arranging the colors in a random fashion (figure 105). Sew triangle G to this unit. Seam the dark A triangle to the pieced triangle (figure 109). Make 28 blocks.
2. Seam the blocks together in horizontal rows of

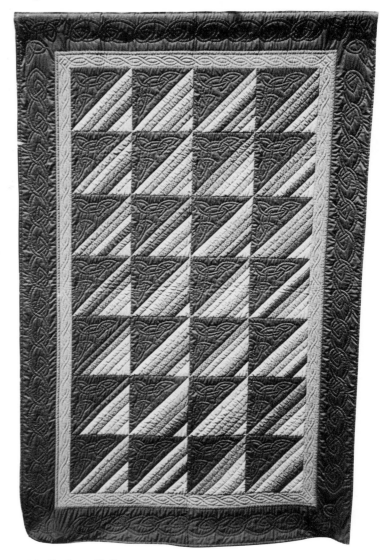

104. Shadows Quilt.

four blocks each. Then sew the seven rows together to form the pieced area of the quilt top.
3. Sew the 3-inch light-colored border to the pieced area. Then add the 1-inch medium-colored border. Finish with the 6-inch dark border. Press.
4. Mark the quilting designs on the quilt top (figure 106). Start border designs in the corners and ease them to fit in the centers of the borders (figures 107 and 108).
5. Layer. Baste, and put the quilt in a frame. Quilt, following the marked pattern.
6. Bind with the dark solid fabric. Finish with a personalized label.

ENLARGE AND ADD ¼" SEAM ALLOWANCE.

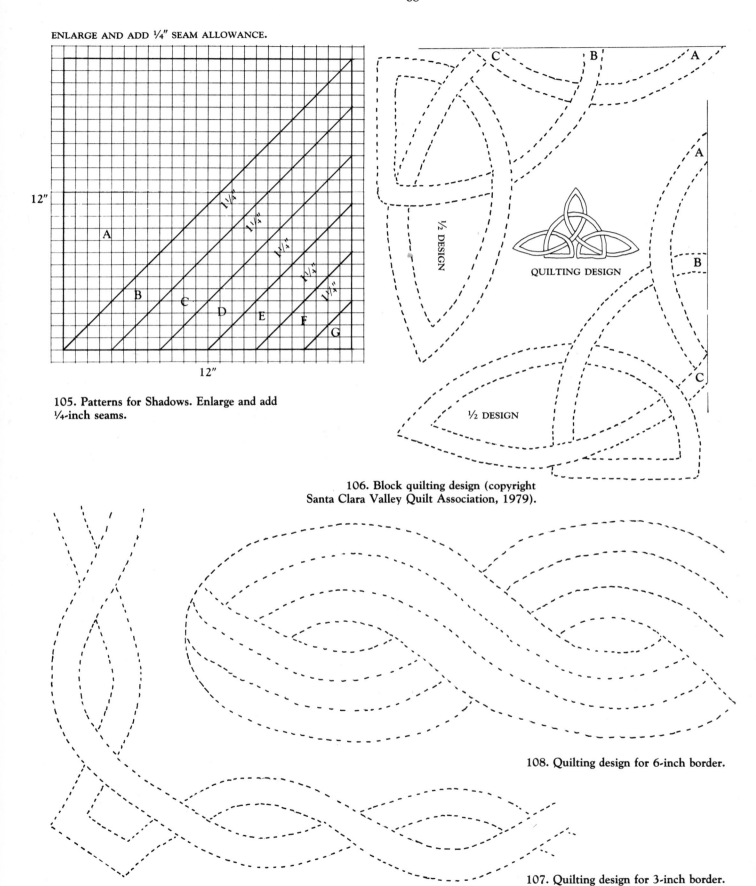

105. Patterns for Shadows. Enlarge and add ¼-inch seams.

106. Block quilting design (copyright Santa Clara Valley Quilt Association, 1979).

108. Quilting design for 6-inch border.

107. Quilting design for 3-inch border.

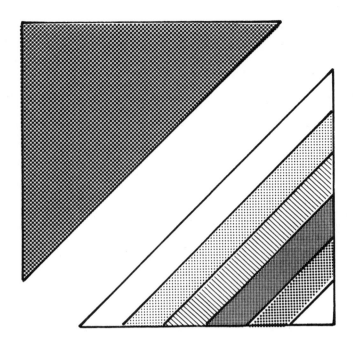

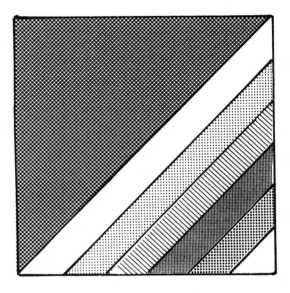

109. Assembling the Shadows block pieces.

OHIO STAR QUILT

Ohio Star is one of the most versatile of the traditional patterns. Our version is set with sashes, but the quilt will take on a completely different look without them, when the interplay of patterns is encouraged by a solid set. This particular quilt boasts a Wild Goose Chase border and half-size stars in the corners. It's large—a generous 87 inches by 102 inches, big enough for a queen-size bed. This is an ideal intermediate project for the group with some experience.

Quilt size: 87″ x 102″
Block size: 12″ (set 4 x 5 with 3″ sashes)
Sash size (without seam allowance): 3″
Border sizes (without seam allowances):
 muslin borders 1½″
 Wild Goose Chase border 6″
 print border 1″
 dark solid border 2″
Yardage (44″ fabric):
 muslin 3 yds.
 dark solid 3 yds.
 print 3 yds.
 backing 6 yds.
 batting 89″ x 104″
Quilt requires: 20 A blocks; 4 B blocks; 98 C blocks.

Each A block requires:
 muslin 4A;
 dark solid 1A, 8B;
 print 4B.
Each B block requires:
 muslin 4A;
 dark solid 1A, 8B;
 print 4B.
Each C block requires:
 dark solid 2E;
 print 1D.
Techniques: machine or hand piecing; hand quilting.
Degree of difficulty: Intermediate.

110. Ohio Star.

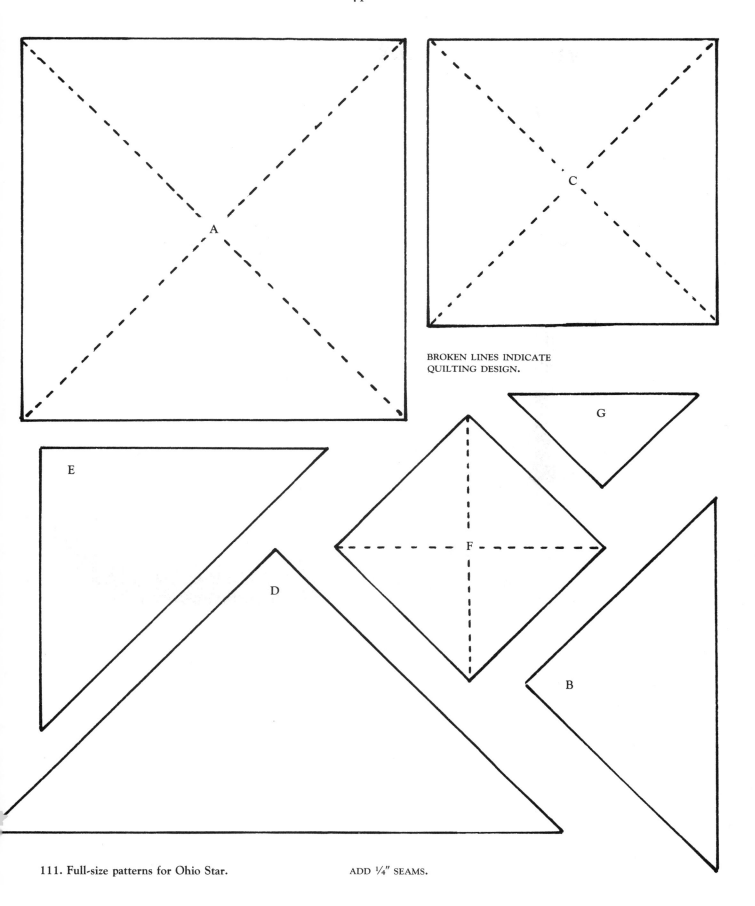

BROKEN LINES INDICATE
QUILTING DESIGN.

111. Full-size patterns for Ohio Star.   ADD ¼″ SEAMS.

ASSEMBLY

1. First, piece all of the A blocks (figure 112). Sew a print B piece to a solid B piece, then a solid B to a muslin B; seam these two units together (figure 113). Assemble the A blocks in three horizontal rows (figure 114). Make 20 A blocks.

2. Assemble the B blocks, which are miniature A blocks. Using pattern pieces F and G, and following the piecing directions above, sew 4 B blocks.

3. Block C is the Wild Goose Chase block. (Note that pattern piece E is *not* the same as pattern piece B. Mark these similar templates clearly so they are not accidentally interchanged.) Sew a solid E to a print D; then sew on the second solid E patch (figure 115). Seam two rows of 22 Wild Goose Chase blocks for the top and bottom borders of the quilt; seam two rows of 27 Wild Goose Chase blocks for the sides.

4. From the 3-inch print sashing fabric, cut two strips 12½ inches long and sew to the right and left sides of each Ohio Star block. These form the vertical sashes.

5. Now for the horizontal sashes: Piece a dark solid C square to a 12½-inch length of the printed sash fabric. Alternate solid squares and printed sash strips (figure 116) until you have made six strips composed of 5 squares and 4 sashes. Pin these in place and assemble the quilt in horizontal rows, referring to the photo for guidance.

6. Sew on the 1½-inch muslin border.

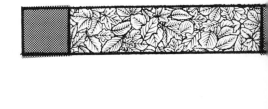

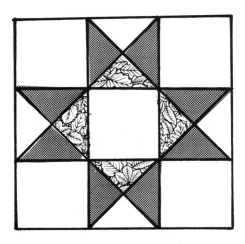

112. Finished 12-inch A block.

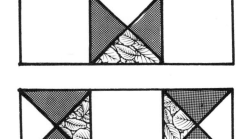

113. Assembling first pieces for A block.

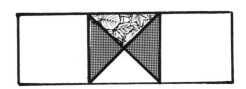

114. Assembling rows to finish A block.

115. Assembling the C block.

7. Sew the 27-unit Wild Goose Chase borders to the right and left sides of the quilt.

8. Sew the miniature Ohio Star blocks to the ends of the remaining Wild Goose Chase borders. Seam these borders in place at the top and bottom of the quilt.

9. Add another 1½-inch muslin border. Then, sew on a 1-inch border of the print fabric. Finish the quilt top with a 2-inch border of the solid fabric. Press.

10. Seam the backing together. Layer. Baste, and put the quilt into a frame. Quilt diagonals in the 2-, 3-, and 4-inch squares (see broken lines on the pattern pieces for guidance). Outline-quilt the Wild Goose Chase blocks. "Meander"-quilt the sashes and borders: First, draw a freehand wandering line through the borders, or else lay a length of yarn along the borders, draping it into irregular curves; then trace around these curves, and remove the yarn. If you would prefer regular curves, trace one-third of a round plastic lid or similar template (figure 117).

11. Bind the quilt in the dark solid. Finish with a signature or label.

116. Horizontal sash.

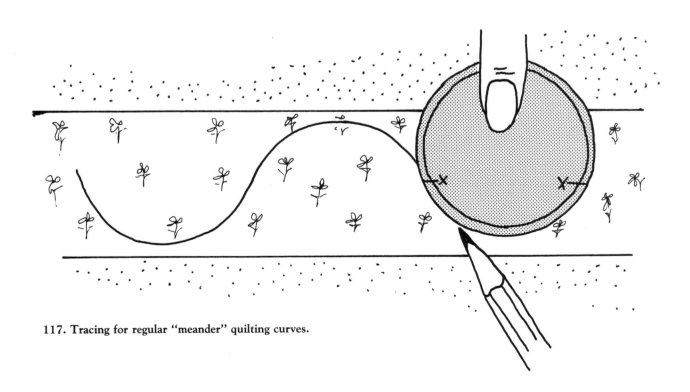

117. Tracing for regular "meander" quilting curves.

PROPELLER QUILT

Here is another easy design set on the diagonal. When one quilt club made this design, they chose muslin and a lively print for the squares. Then each member contributed scraps from her own collection for the large triangles. An interesting mix of fabrics gives this quilt an old-fashioned charm. The design is quick to piece and easy to sew by machine. Hand quilting in a curving propeller design finishes this lovely quilt in a most appropriate way.

ASSEMBLY

1. To make A blocks, sew four muslin B triangles to four scrap B triangles; then sew four muslin A squares to four primary-print A squares (figure 120). Assemble the blocks in three horizontal rows (figure 121), then join the rows (figure 122). Make 49 A blocks.

2. From the primary print, cut 22 border blocks from the C template. To make the corner blocks, sew two C's together as shown in figure 123. Make 4 corner blocks.

3. Assemble the quilt in diagonal rows, using the photograph as a guide for block placement. Press well.

4. Mark the curving propeller design on the finished quilt top. Place the design at the intersections of the blocks (figure 124).

5. Sew the backing together. Layer. Baste, and put the quilt into a frame. Outline-quilt the center squares and quilt the curving propellers.

6. Bind and finish with a signature or label.

Quilt size: 71″ x 85″

Block size: 10″ (set diagonally in alternating 4-block, 5-block rows for 11 rows)

Yardage (44″ fabric):

muslin	2½ yds.
primary print	2½ yds.
scraps or secondary print(s)	2 yds.
backing	5 yds.
batting	73″ x 87″

Quilt requires: 49 A blocks; 22 (10″) triangles cut from the primary print using template C.

Each A block requires:

muslin	5A, 4B;
primary print	4A;
scraps	4B.

Techniques: machine or hand piecing; hand quilting.

Degree of difficulty: easy.

118. Propeller.

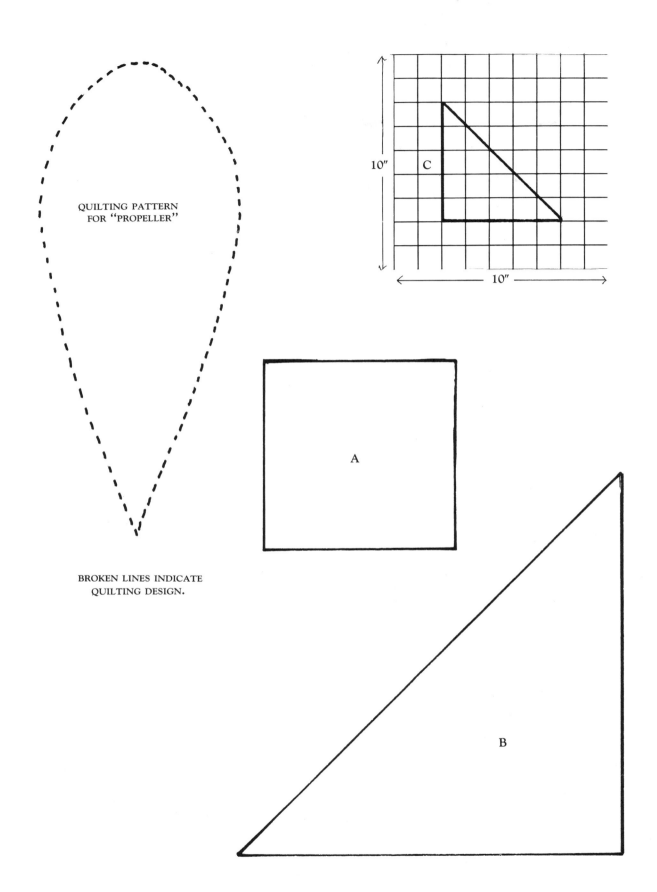

QUILTING PATTERN
FOR "PROPELLER"

BROKEN LINES INDICATE
QUILTING DESIGN.

10″

10″

C

A

B

**119. Full-size patterns
for Propeller.**   ADD ¼″ SEAMS.

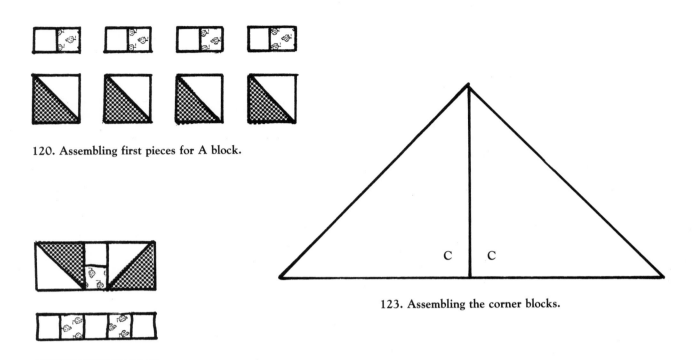

120. Assembling first pieces for A block.

123. Assembling the corner blocks.

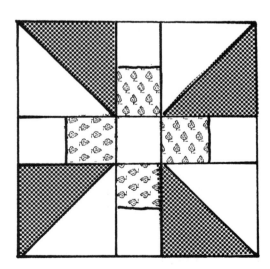

121. Assembling rows to
finish A block.

124. Intersection of four blocks,
over which propeller quilting design
is applied.

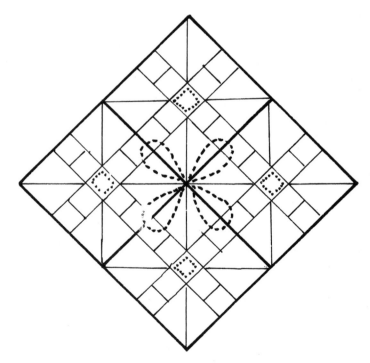

122. Finished 10-inch A block.

A Guide to Cooperative Quiltmaking

Although our own experiences coordinating cooperative quilts had been fun, successful, and personally enriching, we knew there were others who had had less positive experiences. So we sought out and listened carefully to several discouraged women. Some complained about putting in an inordinate amount of time while others loafed. Some disliked the chosen design or objected to poor needlework. More than a few said that their projects had nearly failed because of naive mistakes in calculating time or materials. Still others wrote to say that although their quilts had come out fine they would never make another because the whole project had been so beset with difficulties—finding people to work, and coordinating time, energy, and funds.

I am in Stage Four of group quiltmaking. Stage One is, "Oh, wouldn't it be a great idea to make a quilt for So-and-So!" Stage Two is batting around the theme. Stage Three is getting excited, buying the material, people coming out of the woodwork to help. Stage Four is, "Why in blue blazes did we ever *think* of anything like this? Never again! If everyone involved will only go on being my friend, I'll be happy. Where did all those quilters go—back into the woodwork?

Anonymous

We have thought long and hard about why some groups achieve triumphant successes and why others feel they've failed. The critical factor seems to be planning, first for the people and then for the quilt. It is natural for all of us to be swept up in an initial burst of enthusiasm, but if the project is to succeed, we need to plan carefully. The people always come first in our plans, because without them we do not have a project.

Planning for the Group: Gathering the People, Assessing Skills, Deepening the Commitment

One young, inexperienced quiltmaker wanted to make a bicentennial quilt to honor her community. She solicited people to help her by placing a classified ad in the newspaper. Thirty women answered her ad, and she assigned them appliqué squares. When the squares were returned, she sashed the quilt, basted it, and quilted it herself. When the quilt was completed, there was no hoopla, no party, no celebration. The local museum was pleased to receive it but not prepared to stage an event. The young coordinator couldn't help but feel alone, let down, and strangely unfulfilled after this unceremonious reception, considering she had just produced such a lovely creation. Some planning for the human element of her project could very well have transformed her experience.

Jackie Dodson from La Grange Park, Illinois, wrote us this account of her group experience:

I've given a lot of thought to why this quilt was so successful. For one thing, it bonded the women of the church in a way that nothing else ever had before. Sunday mornings were all quilt talk. Everyone was stitching and comparing and sharing. We wanted our work to be superb. Coffees were hastily called, and everyone brought her stitching. The bottom line is that we were making this surprise quilt for someone we and our kids loved dearly. When we hired Dave to be the as-

sistant pastor, we got a gem. There wasn't one woman who talked to me about what the quilt meant who didn't mention how much she loved Dave. So I believe that our gratitude and love were the magic ingredients.

The thing that brings group quilters together, the common bond, could be their mutual love for the person who is to receive the quilt. But it could also be sharing a common cause, like the peace quilts (see page 17) or the quilts donated to the Ronald McDonald Houses (see page 22). Perhaps they all share strong connections to a group they belong to, or to a special place, or a person they all admire. Sometimes the common bond is simply the desire to learn to quilt or to get to know other people better by working on a project together. If each quilter understands what the common connections are and how the project grows logically out of those connections, it will be easy for her to decide to fully support the project with her time and talent.

Each quilter needs to feel that this is *her* project. This kind of commitment comes from plenty of dis-

Questions for the Initial Discussion

1. What are our reasons for making this quilt? Will it be a gift, a learning project, a fundraiser, a commemorative quilt?

2. How skilled are we? Do our talents vary a great deal? What are our strong and weak areas? (Include both sewing skills and other useful assets like teaching, record keeping, coordinating, photography, design, drawing, and so on.) Will we use this project to learn new techniques? Can/should we be satisfied with uneven or imperfect work in our finished quilt? Will we work by hand or machine, or both?

3. Who will be the coordinator? Will it be one person or more than one? What will her responsibilities be? (Suggestions for this role follow.)

4. Will we need written directions, precut kits, or teaching workshops? How will we provide for these? Do we need a telephone tree or mailing system to contact each person easily and rapidly?

5. How much time are people willing to contribute to this project? Does this seem

like enough? Can people contribute varying amounts of time without causing resentment in the group? What is a realistic deadline? How long are we willing to take to make this quilt?

6. How many people will help? Is this enough? Is this too many? What will we do if we have "extra" people, or people who drop out, or people who want to join after we have started?

7. Who will pay for the materials?

8. Where will we work? How far apart do we live? Does distance create any special considerations? Is there a large, convenient place to quilt together? Is there someone who will lend a frame?

9. How will this quilt be used? How does the use affect our choice of materials, or methods of construction?

10. Do we have any special needs? (These might include keeping the quilt a secret, incorporating unusual fabrics, meeting a strict deadline, designing a quilt for a specific space, making a quilt to frame or hang, or needing to raise money through the sale of the quilt.)

cussion at the beginning of the project. Everyone needs a chance to express her own feelings and ideas about the proposed quilt and to get some sense of what her role will be. The initial meeting and discussion are also important for setting the atmosphere for the group. We have prepared the accompanying list of questions to help focus and guide this first meeting. Some of the questions will help the organizer refine her ideas; others will let her assess the skills and resources of the members. As the group works through the questions together, the process of discussing ideas and eventually arriving at concensus will help build a healthy, cohesive collection of people.

The initial meeting usually produces a rush of excitement, and people will leave the meeting enthusiastic and eager to begin. But occasionally, for one reason or another, the muses of enthusiasm and commitment will not grace that meeting with their presence. If this is the case, we strongly suggest shelving the whole idea and trying again later when the conditions may be better. Pressing a reluctant group into making a quilt is sure to lead to bitterness and disappointment. If the initial meeting is hopeful, but people are reticent about making their commitments (as is often the case when the group is comprised of strangers), schedule a second, group-building meeting. Teaching workshops are an especially good way to cement relationships within a cautious group. They allow people time to get a feel for working with the others, as well as time to explore sewing and quiltmaking skills. The color-palette exercise described in chapter 2 is another possibility for a noncommitted group's second meeting.

Dividing Up the Work

Once an enthusiastic, committed group has established itself, it will be time to divide up the work of making the quilt. Since every group is unique, there is no one construction plan that will work for everyone. Some groups like to have a different co-ordinator for design, construction, publicity, and raffle; others prefer a simpler format, with one co-ordinator to oversee all the activities. Yet another group may function best with a pair of friends serving as coordinators. Some groups work quickly, producing their quilts in as few as six sessions. Others have taken more than a year to complete their projects.

The initial meeting will offer some sense of the scope of the project and who will participate. Then the coordinator and a small committee will rough out a master plan: They will list the jobs, filling in possible names and a time schedule. Although some names will change as volunteers step forward, the original list will nevertheless be a good indicator of how much support there is and where more help is needed. The committee should present this master plan while the plan is still rough and open to ideas and changes from the group. This plan will grow organically out of specific needs, shaping itself to individual circumstances; no "packaged" plan we could offer here would work as well. But do use the following chronological job list as the basis for the master plan. Detailed job descriptions follow.

Quilt Jobs
- Coordinating
- Designing the quilt and drafting the patterns
- Estimating time, cost, and yardage
- Giving directions
- Buying fabric
- Cutting
- Sewing
- Marking for quilting
- Basting
- Quilting
- Binding, labeling, and preparing for hanging

Other Jobs
- Coordinating raffle/auction
- Coordinating telephone
- Teaching workshops
- Photography
- Arranging publicity
- Documenting the project by keeping records
- Thanking participants and celebrating the work

QUILT JOBS

If there are greatly varying skills and originality in the group, the finished quilt may appear uneven, mixing elaborately embroidered masterpieces with more humble blocks whose best attributes are their intentions. Like Grandma's featherbed, cooperative

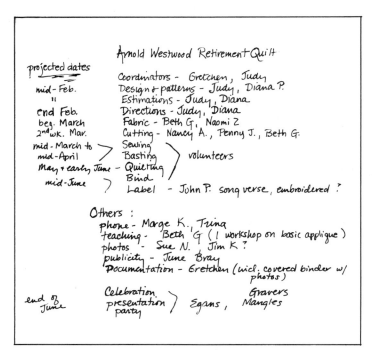

Arnold Westwood Retirement Quilt

projected dates
mid-Feb.   Coordinators - Gretchen, Judy
    "   Design & patterns - Judy, Diana P.
end Feb.   Estimations - Judy, Diana
beg. March   Directions - Judy, Diana
2nd wk. Mar.   Fabric - Beth G, Naomi Z
    Cutting - Nancy A., Penny J., Beth G.
mid-March to   Sewing
mid-April   Basting } volunteers
May + early June - Quilting
mid-June   Bind
    Label - John P. song verse, embroidered?

Others :
    phone - Marge K., Trina
    teaching - Beth G (1 workshop on basic applique)
    photos - Sue N., Jim K?
    publicity - June Bray
    Documentation - Gretchen (incl. covered binder w/ photos)

end of June   Celebration, presentation party } Egans, Gravers Mangles

125. Sample: a roughed-out master plan ready to be presented to the group for refinement.

quilts need to make room for everybody. Experienced sewers deserve a chance to showcase their talents, and beginners need a place to practice, so plan ahead for this. The work need not be divided block by block, however. Beginners can work a pieced sashing; simpler "filler" blocks can be used alternately with more elaborate blocks; or beginners and experts can work together on the same blocks. Or everyone may decide to live with it, accepting the unevenness as a valid statement about the identity of the group. We asked the Congregational Church women of Portland, Connecticut, how they managed to create their lovely medallion quilt, even though it includes 46 six-inch Mariner's Compass blocks (see figure 16). It appears flawlessly even, more like the work of one experienced quilter than that of a diverse group of amateurs. They told us their "secret": their talented teacher, Carolyn Johnson. Carolyn and Joy Rutty designed the quilt and pieced the difficult center section. The rest of the blocks were distributed among the others in the group, and, despite good-natured groans of protest, each woman was able to complete her blocks under Carolyn's tutelage.

THE COORDINATOR'S ROLE

As key person, the coordinator maintains an overview. She directs the work being done and keeps track of what needs to happen next. She should be diplomatic, flexible, comfortable with her own responsibilities yet eager to delegate work whenever possible, knowing that this project belongs to everyone. Her sense of humor buoys her through the absurd, unforeseeable circumstances that inevitably arise whenever any group takes on a common task. Besides sharing many of these traits, good coordinators can be most diverse. Some are expert quilters, but a few do not quilt at all. Some have aggressive managerial styles, while others maintain a low profile and quietly guide the project. Some coordinators spend a great deal of time at their jobs; others efficiently squeeze their responsibilities into weekday lunch hours.

Your group might prefer to have the coordinator's role shared by two people who enjoy working together. One way to do this is to choose a coordinator and let her name her own assistant. But the coordinator's job cannot be performed efficiently by a committee.

Occasionally a group will balk at choosing a coordinator. When this happens, it is important to ask why. Is it a small group that has made cooperative quilts before and already knows the steps they want to take? Is the group reluctant to single out one person as having more leadership or organizational skills than the rest? Is there no one who wants to put in the necessary effort? Unless someone assumes the coordinator's role, the responsibility will fall on everyone. This means that each person has to keep track of the whole project—an awkward, complicated situation. We feel it is far better to name a coordinator than to beg the issue and let the responsibility fall willy-nilly to whomever happens along.

DESIGN AND PATTERN DRAFTING

The first thing people will notice about the quilt is its design. In the beginning, the entire group can be involved in the designing process by offering ideas, themes, layout and color schemes. But after everyone has had a chance to contribute, the actual design is best left to one or two volunteers.

The job of the designer is to synthesize the group's ideas and produce an appropriate result. Although it will not be possible to incorporate everyone's ideas, allowing the group to inspire with suggestions makes it possible to interpret their ideas as one sees fit. If the group has already made some clear design decisions, the designer's job is then to devise an imaginative set for their patchwork or applique blocks.

The designer makes a scaled drawing of the quilt on graph paper. This is the design plan. Figure 126 shows Barbara Wysocki's plan for Nanny's Album Quilt (see page 27). It is wise to keep this in a safe place or to make a few photocopies, since it will be referred to often. Measurements should be noted directly on the drawing, which is also used for determining yardage. (The drawing will serve as a handy reference for block placement as well.) Careful preparation of the design plan averts many disasters. It will indicate if a pieced border will not turn a corner or if a repeating pattern will not resolve. Once all is ready for devising the quilting design, trial designs can be sketched on sheets of tracing paper placed over the graph-paper design plan.

The designer is responsible for drafting accurate templates. To reduce the chance of a drafting error, this should be done by one person, who will then cut and piece one trial block out of scrap fabric to check for accuracy and to serve as a model.

Bearing in mind the wishes of the group, the designer also devises a color scheme. In a small, established group, the designer will often be entrusted with selecting the colors and fabrics herself, and the members will abide by her decision. In a larger or less established group, however, the designer may choose to present two or three color schemes and let a vote decide the issue.

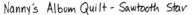

Nanny's Album Quilt - Sawtooth Star

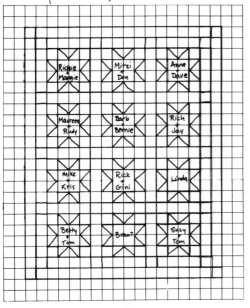

overall dimensions : 54" x 69"

Block size : 12"
sashes : 3"
borders : 3"

Yardage :
muslin - 1 yd.
scraps - 1 yd.
(red)
navy - 1¼ yd.
print - 1 yd.

backing - 3½ yds.

126. Sample design plan.

ESTIMATING TIME, COST, AND YARDAGE

Judy coordinated the Snail Trail Quilt (see figure 79) for a church raffle; it was completed in fewer than 70 hours by 10 women. This quilt, machine pieced and hand quilted, was a real quickie. Gretchen, on the other hand, estimates that 750 hours went into making the Teachers' Centers Quilt (see C-20 in color section). But even this figure is not so overwhelming when you realize that 50 participants needed to contribute only 15 hours each to make the total.

The job of estimating time, cost, and yardage will belong to the coordinator and the designer. If neither is a seasoned quilter, it will be necessary to include an experienced quiltmaker or two in these decisions.

Consider the following factors when estimating time:

- **Number of people.** Too few people make for a slow project; too many become unwieldy and also slow down progress.
- **Experience.** A group of experienced needle women work faster than do a group of beginners. An established group works faster than do a group of strangers.
- **Deadlines.** People will take as long as they're given to produce their block, so set a reasonable deadline, and decide how to deal with blocks that come in late.
- **Technique.** Patchwork is usually faster than appliqué. Lots of intricate quilting takes time.
- **Distance.** If people are mailing blocks from afar, allow plenty of extra time.
- **Calendar year.** Some people will not be able to work during holiday and vacation seasons; others will have more time then.

With fabric prices at about $4 per yard, the average quilt costs anywhere from $75 to $100. Clever planning may reduce the cost dramatically, but it is surprisingly easy to spend more than $100. In estimating your costs, consider a number of factors:

- **Size.** Small quilts cost less to make than do big quilts.
- **Fabric price.** Groups occasionally will be given discounts on yard goods.
- **Incidentals.** In addition to fabric for the top, batting, backing fabric, thread, and perhaps marking pencils, templates, and other notions will be needed.

◆ **Donations.** Such contributions will decrease costs. Besides the quilt shop owner, civic groups and local businesses that have an interest in a group's cause can be approached for cash donations to defray expenses.

◆ **Services.** Some groups hire a paid coordinator. Additional expenses may also include fees paid to workshop teachers or for an artist's design, or for photocopying, photography, postage, and rental of opaque projectors or other equipment.

Just as we have our preferred methods for estimating time and cost, almost all experienced quilters will have a favorite way of estimating yardage. This simple, visually oriented system works for us: Imagine a 45-inch width of fabric unfurling off into infinity. Walk along it for three yards, then cut across its width; proceed another three yards and cut an identical piece. Place these two pieces side by side, and you have enough fabric to cover a twin bed. A total of six yards of fabric was necessary. For larger beds, or for the quilt to hang to the floor, extra widths will be needed. Long beds may require that each width be longer than the three yards. The measurements of commercial bedcovers can serve as guides if a particular size is required for a project.

We calculate the yardage for the pieced or appliquéd top by estimating in percents. Taking a look at the block design (or a sketch of a typical appliqué block), determine what percent of the block is blue. Is it approximately 10 percent? 25 percent? 50 percent? What percent is red? yellow? If 50 percent of each block of a twin-bed quilt is red, and we know that it takes six yards to cover a twin bed, then three yards of red will be needed. Add an extra half-yard to cover seams and minor errors, and buy three and a half yards. If 25 percent of each block is yellow, then figure 25 percent of six yards—one and a half yards—plus an extra quarter-yard for safety, and buy one and three-quarters yards. Mathematically inclined persons will find alternate estimating methods in Michael James's *Quiltmaker's Handbooks*. Not being particularly mathematical ourselves, we also appreciate Bonnie Leman and Judy Martin's book, *Taking the Math Out of Making Patchwork Quilts*.

EXTRA EXTRA EXTRA EXTRA EXTRA

When making estimates, always allow extra: extra time, money, yardage, and quilt blocks. Unforeseen happenings are sure to occur, and having a small reserve of time, cash, or blue calico can rescue a group later. If one is an experienced quiltmaker skilled at estimating her own projects, she would do well to be particularly careful to pad those estimates for group projects. The same quilt made by a group will use more fabric than if it were made by an individual, because the possibilities for error increase proportionately to the size of the group.

GIVING DIRECTIONS

The coordinator and designer together usually provide directions for the group. These directions need to be clearly presented so that people know what is expected of them. It is a good idea to issue printed handouts. In addition to specific information about what to do and how to do it, the directions should include the name and phone number of a person who can help with technical problems and answer questions, as well as the due date and the name of the person collecting the finished blocks.

Sally Arciolo agreed to let us reproduce her directions (figure 127) for the Bowers Museum Quilt. She is clear and specific, and at the same time helps everyone keep the overall effect in mind by instructing her sewers to keep the basic shapes simple, striving for a primitive feeling. Other good direction sheets may be more detailed than Sally's, but before they reach book-length proportions, one might consider organizing a teaching workshop or recommending already published books for the group to read.

BUYING FABRIC

It seems obvious to us that a dozen people cannot go shopping together, but we heard of one group that did just that. After several hours of rearranging the bolts in a large quilt shop, they finally came to a consensus. This in itself is a remarkable tribute to the good nature of these women, but we feel the real tribute here should go to the quilt shop owner! Our advice is to send a very small delegation to do the shopping. One person should then wash, dry, and iron the fabric to remove extra dye, sizing, and wrinkles.

CUTTING

This job includes marking, cutting the fabric, and dividing it into kits if necessary. It, too, is best accomplished by a small committee. One careful person doing all the tracing and cutting will achieve the greatest accuracy, but we find this such a tedious job that we would dread having to do it alone; rather, this would make a good job for two or three friends—preferably those with tendencies toward

BOWERS MUSEUM SHOP

BOWERS MUSEUM SHOP ETHNIC QUILT PROJECT

Sat. June 26 10:00am — First Group Meeting: Fabric passed out; countries chosen, general guidelines discussed.

Sat. July 19 10:00am — Second Group Meeting: Present designs. Technical and design help will be avilable; suggestions may be made on the individual blocks to enhance the overall design.

Sat. August 14 — Finished squares are due. Turn in to the Bowers Museum Shop.

Please call for advice, encouragement or answers to questions:

Nancy Fister, museum shop manager 999-9999(shop) 999-9999(home)

Sally Arcolio, quilt coordinator 999-9999(home)

GENERAL GUIDELINES

Sewing concerns

1. The 13 inch square of unbleached muslin is your background fabric. The finished square is 12 inches, leaving a 1/2 inch seam allowance.
2. All work must be done by hand; no machine applique.
3. All raw edges must be turned under--and please no fusible web or adhesives.
4. You may add details or embellishments with embroidery using only shades of the colors in the fabric. Check with Sally for the floss numbers.

Design and color use concerns

5. For ease in applique, keep the basic shapes of your design fairly simple with rather a primitive feeling. Try for an impression rather than a realistic depiction of your selection.
6. Make your design cover a minimum of 2/3 of the square. It need not extend out to the seam allowance, but it may if it suits your design.
7. All the squares must include some use of the mulberry leaf print--the rest is up to you.
8. The sashing fabric is the solid mulberry broadcloth. Do not use it where it will touch the sashing border.
9. The pink and bright turquoise print are the accent fabrics. Please use them in relatively small amounts.
10. Experiment with the fabrics. Use your imagination in design and fabric selection. Trust your feelings--enjoy yourself!

Sally says: "Please call me anytime if you have a question or problem."

2002 N. Main St. • Santa Ana • California • 92706 • (714) 558-1133

127. Sample of group directions.

compulsive neatness. Pairs of cutters working together are more likely to catch each other's mistakes.

Borders and sashes should be cut out first from the continuous yardage so that these long strips remain relatively seamless. The cutters should then make up the kits block by block, being sure to mark the fabric pieces if a grain line is critical. The kits usually go into plastic bags along with any printed directions; they are then distributed by the cutters for sewing.

SEWING

There are three sewing jobs: sewing the individual blocks; sewing the blocks (and sashing) together to make the top; and sewing the backing into one piece. If clear directions have been given, most experienced quilters will be able to sew their blocks at home. Many times this will be the best way to proceed, but we encourage sewing together as a group as often as possible. People are able to compare their work and learn from what others are doing. Valuable self-correcting takes place when people work together, and this spares the coordinator from assuming the role of teacher. Working together also ensures a more unified quilt as people alter their blocks to make them conform to the work of the others.

In spite of the best instructions and intentions, some blocks may still come in poorly sewn. If the quilt is a gift for an individual or a family member, the better course may be to leave these blocks alone. If the quilt is to be sold, however, or if it is specifically made for display, then the poorly sewn blocks will have to be reworked. Sometimes an inadequate block can be subjected to a little invisible reinforcement performed quietly and discreetly by the coordinator. At other times, the coordinator will have to approach the quilter with the problem. Usually if it is stated as a problem and not a crime, the improvements can be negotiated without any hurt feelings.

Sewing the finished blocks together to make the top of the quilt is a pleasant job for three to five friends. This can be efficiently organized so that the pinning, sewing, and pressing take place in assembly-line fashion. Consulting the original design plan ensures that each block is sewn into its proper place. The sewers finish the top by pressing it carefully. When they have sewn the backing fabric together, their job is complete.

MARKING FOR QUILTING

Many quilts are outline quilted following the pieced or appliqué designs. It is not necessary to mark these quilts. Other quilts employ elaborate quilting as a design element, and it is best to mark these on the quilt top before it is layered and basted. This job can be quite time consuming if an intricate quilting pattern is chosen. Usually, two or three people will be able to mark an average quilt in a few hours.

BASTING

Layering and basting a quilt is a job that eight or more people can do at once. Many hands are really a help with this task, straightening, smoothing, threading the long basting needles, and putting in the basting stitches. This is almost always a floor exercise, awkwardly accomplished crawling around on all fours. People's tolerance for this kind of activity is low, so plan to have plenty of volunteers and finish in one session. A few rather expensive quilt frames claim to eliminate basting. Experimenting with one of these may be fun for your group. Large tables provide another alternative to floor basting; Ping-Pong tables or folding banquet tables pushed together will suffice. Once finished, the basters may put the quilt into the frame, or else this may be delegated to the first group of quilters.

QUILTING

Even very large quilts can be quilted in a hoop, passing them around from home to home, one person quilting at a time. But we greatly prefer the large floor-frame traditionally used at quilting bees, one that allows six or more people to quilt at once. Quilting progresses quickly at a large frame, and the rhythmic, repetitive work is relaxing and conducive to good conversation. Many people have written to say that the conversations at their quilting frames led to new friendships as well as new insights into old friends.

BINDING, LABELING, AND HANGING

After the quilt is removed from the frame, it will need to be trimmed and bound along the edges. This is a one-day job for two friends. When the binding is done, they will attach the label to the quilt (see later in this chapter for more about labels). If there is a possibility that the quilt will be hung, they will sew a casing along the top of the back of the quilt. A wooden firring strip with holes at each end can be slipped into the casing, allowing the quilt to hang securely supported (figure 128).

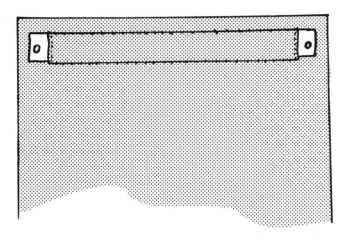

128. Back of quilt, showing casing and firring strip for hanging.

OTHER JOBS

The tasks above produce the quilt. But it is the other jobs—the photography, publicity, workshops, phone calls, and celebrations—that add an elegance and the sort of personal touch that can transform a project from being an "okay experience" to a "quilting high." We briefly outline those jobs here to encourage an early lining up of volunteers. Later in this chapter appears an in-depth description of how these additional activities can enhance your project.

COORDINATING A RAFFLE OR AUCTION

The job of setting up a quilt raffle or auction is so substantial that it requires a separate coordinator and its own time schedule that begins long before the quilt is finished. The coordinator of a quilt should not be expected to take on this job too. The raffle/auction coordinator must have a real appreciation of the quilt, because his or her enthusiasm will be a major factor in how much money the quilt earns. This coordinator will be in charge of obtaining permits, having tickets printed and distributed, keeping track of money, setting up a drawing or auction site, and finding a suitable person to be auctioneer or pick the winning ticket. He or she will have to decide on a reasonable financial goal and set a minimum bid or number of tickets to be sold. There is plenty of work here for two people, so co-coordinators would be appropriate in this case, too.

TELEPHONING

Phone calls can be coordinated by one person, or they can be divided among several people. A telephone tree is perfect for a group effort of this kind. During quilt construction, calls will help gather people for work meetings, check progress and see if help is needed, and remind people of approaching deadlines. During raffles, people may need to be contacted about selling tickets, and later about returning unsold tickets and stubs.

TEACHING WORKSHOPS

Workshops to teach skills, spark ideas, and build enthusiasm may be scheduled before the quilt is started, as well as during the construction of the blocks and in the early stages of quilting.

PHOTOGRAPHY

A volunteer who is adept with a camera should take pictures of the quilt in progress. Several groups have made slide shows about the making of their quilt for their celebration, and for use by school and community groups. Photographs of the finished quilt will be valuable for insurance records, publicity, ticket sales, and sharing with friends who live far away. Be sure to take both color slides and black-and-white prints if there is any chance that the quilt will be entered in a show or reproduced in a book, or pictured on posters or postcards.

PUBLICITY

Look for an enthusiastic person to handle the publicity for the quilt. This person need not be a quilter; a knowledgeable supporter is fine. If the quilt is to be a fundraiser, publicity is critically important; perhaps in this case more than one person should share this job. The publicity person or committee will see that posters are made and distributed to announce fundraising intentions. They will prepare press releases for the local newspapers and announcements for public-service spots on local radio and television. Their promotion activities will give a large number of people the opportunity to buy raffle tickets or consider an auction bid.

DOCUMENTATION

Most groups have at least one person who likes to make scrapbooks or keep journals. A well-documented project will make any subsequent quilt a lot easier and will allow this project to serve as a model for others.

CELEBRATIONS AND THANK-YOUS

Do not leave this job to the people who have had the lion's share of the quilting work—they are the ones whose work most particularly needs to be celebrated, and they should not have to organize their own thank-yous. A small party should be planned to thank the quilters when they have finished the quilt; another celebration may be in order when the quilt is presented to its new owners. Include far-away friends by sending letters and a photograph of the festivities.

Alternatives to Traditional Construction of Cooperative Quilts

Today's quilters have devised many variations on the traditional system of quilt construction. The Tips section at the end of this chapter offers additional valuable ideas that can be incorporated into any construction method.

QUILT-AS-YOU-GO

Of all the various quiltmaking techniques, none is more hotly debated than quilt-as-you-go. In this method, the *individual* blocks are layered, basted, and quilted before being joined. Sewing the pre-quilted blocks together can be tedious, and if the blocks are not quite uniform in size, can cause nail biting, hair pulling, and other overt signs of stress.

We have made two group quilts by the quilt-as-you-go method. The first part of the work went well and on time, but we just hated sewing the blocks together. We didn't think we had as worthwhile a finished quilt, either. It always seems that the same workers get left with sewing the blocks together.

Fay Goldey, Rockville, Maryland

Quilt-as-you-go has both good and bad points. We felt that having each person do her own quilting let her have more control over her own design.

Millie Dunkel, Carbondale, Illinois

The Eastern Long Island Quilter's Guild chose quilt-as-you-go for another reason:

The biggest problem to overcome with our last quilt was the distance between guild members. Many travel over an hour to reach our monthly meetings, crossing canals and bays, and several have to take a ferry. Quilt-as-you-go is the only method for such a widely distributed group.

Marlene Haresign, Water Mill, New York

Quilt-as-you-go makes quilting portable, and many people achieve smaller stitches when working on such a manageable piece. The work on each block progresses quickly. On the other hand, what's still left is the monumental job of sewing the quilted blocks together. Another annoying problem with quilt-as-you-go is that individual blocks should not be quilted out to the edge; almost an inch around the perimeter must be left free so that the seams can be sewn. All too often, enthusiastic quilters quilt right up to the edge, making it necessary to pick out those stitches later.

Hazel Carter of Vienna, Virginia, coordinates conventions and quilters' tours. Recently, her group, comprised of women from all over the country, toured Ireland. Later, they made a quilt to record their memories. Like the Eastern Long Island quilters, distance among these quilters prompted Hazel to choose quilt-as-you-go. She tackled the two main quilt-as-you-go problems—blocks that finish slightly off size, and blocks accidently quilted out to the edge—by using a sashing system that minimizes these two bugbears (figure 129).

Marlene Haresign, coordinator of the Appliqué Sampler (see C-14 in color section), set up two bees at which four people worked—two joining sashes by machine, two trimming batting and sewing the backing by hand. Sewing the blocks together by rows allows several people to work at once. Julie Morrison, of the Wings Falls Quilt Guild of Glens Falls, New York, a group with three large quilt-as-you-go projects to their credit offers this:

Most important is to cut the squares to the exact size. We used blue water-erasable pen to mark

129. A sashing method for quilt-as-you-go.

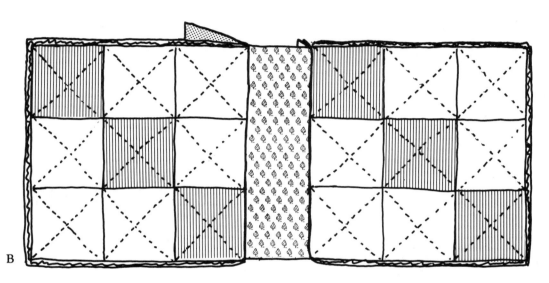

CUT A SASHING STRIP THE SIZE NEEDED, PLUS A
BACKING STRIP TO MATCH. LAY THE BACKING STRIP TO
THE BACK SIDE OF THE BLOCK AND THE SASHING STRIP
TO THE FRONT OF THE BLOCK. STITCH BY MACHINE THROUGH
ALL THE LAYERS. TURN THE STRIPS OUT.

ATTACH THE NEXT BLOCK BY SEWING THE SASHING STRIP TO THE FRONT OF THE BLOCK.

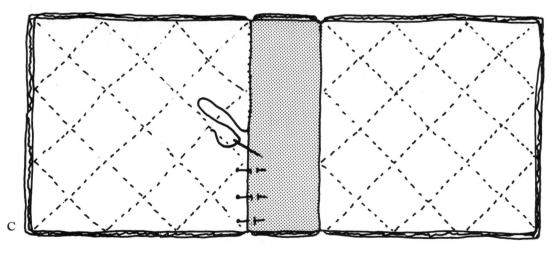

TURN THE BLOCKS OVER AND LAY A STRIP OF BATTING ALONG THE SASH. BRING THE BATTING STRIP
OVER THE BATTING AND WHIPSTITCH DOWN OVER THE SEAM MADE WHEN ATTACHING THE TWO BLOCKS.

the seam lines. We allowed ¼-inch seams on the front and ½-inch seams on the back. It is easier to hand-sew the back with ½-inch seam allowances.

Recutting the batting and getting it to butt properly is a difficult, messy job, almost impossible to get perfect. Borders may make the quilt more attractive, but it's a chore to keep the narrow bands of batting in place. I think wide borders, with quilting to hold the batting in place, are best.

The squares look much better if they are quilted in a small frame.

It is helpful to hand out kits for each block and to spend a day at a workshop putting them together. This helped us solve problems as a group and greatly cut down on phone calls. Though quilt-as-you-go presents problems, we feel that there is a big savings in time. We completed our last quilt in two months.

If you choose quilt-as-you-go, become an expert at it, like Hazel, Marlene, and Julie. *Quilter's Newsletter* publishes a pamphlet about quilt-as-you-go, and variations are offered in *Quick and Easy Quilting* by Bonnie Leman. For our own projects, we try to avoid quilt-as-you-go. We have not found it to be faster than traditional construction, and we also think that the back suffers from this elective surgery—all those extra seams! But mostly we value the opportunity to work closely with others in cohesive groups, and quilt-as-you-go encourages solitary work—even when you're all sitting in the same room.

JUDY'S SPEEDY SYSTEM

Always curious about the possibilities inherent in quilt projects, Judy worked out a system for creating a quilt in six two- or three-hour sessions, using a pool of about ten women. Several of these quick quilts have been raffled to benefit our church. It helps that our congregation is small and the women all know each other, because this system does not allow time at the beginning for building the comraderie of the group. (One or two organizing sessions could easily be added for a less intimate group.)

In this greatly speeded process, the coordinator assumes all responsibility for design and fabric selection, so she should be an experienced quiltmaker trusted by the group who can efficiently design and plan the quilt prior to the first session. This system

works best for fairly simple patchwork patterns with uncomplicated quilting. Color and fabric become the focal point of quick quilts, and so should be chosen imaginatively. The chart on page 89 outlines each person's responsibilities and presents a typical time schedule.

CONTEST QUILTS

One way to obtain blocks for an unusual cooperative quilt is to set up a contest. The Great Things About Pittsburgh Quilt (see C-8 in color section) was the result of such an endeavor, sponsored by the Neighborhoods for Living Center. In most contests, participants are invited to submit blocks that reflect a theme determined by the sponsoring group, and in this case the blocks were to represent Pittsburgh's neighborhoods. The sponsoring group also appoints judges, decides on a color scheme, and perhaps provides fabric. They design a clear entry-form that details prizes and contest rules, including due dates as well as the name and address of a contact person.

Contestants will want to know what will happen to their blocks. If a quilter designs a new block, she automatically owns that design, and if she so wishes, may register it with the federal copyright office. Contest rules should inform contestants whether the sponsoring group is asking for one-time use of the design or if they are also asking for the copyright. A quilter who surrenders the copyright is still free to use the design for private purposes, but may not sell the design or otherwise use it for business purposes, while the new copyright holder is free to use the design in any way—including selling kits or patterns and using it for advertising. Additionally, contestants should be informed how many blocks will be chosen and what the judging criteria will be. If the winning blocks are to be sewn into a quilt, it should be stated who will do this and what the quilt will be used for.

Judging the work of others is serious business. It involves great tact and diplomacy, as well as a discriminating eye and an accepting spirit. The American Crafts Council asks their jurors to make their selections based on originality, imagination, and expertise. *Quilter's Newsletter* publishes a scorecard that clearly defines areas of general appearance, design, and expertise. We feel that there is plenty of room for contests in the field of quiltmaking. Competitions can inspire needleworkers to sharpen their skills and imaginations. Still, contestants need to have resilient egos, because being rejected, no matter how graciously, is hard for all of us.

JUDY'S SPEEDY SYSTEM

Time	Workers	Activity
prior to session 1	coordinator	Choose the pattern. Draft the templates. Sketch the quilt plan. Write directions. Estimate yardage. Buy and wash fabric.
session 1 (2 hours)	coordinator and two others	Cut out the quilt. Divide the fabric into kits by blocks. Distribute the kits. (Blocks are sewn at home by volunteers.)
session 2 (3 hours)	coordinator and 3–4 others	Sew the top together by machine. Press. Cut and sew the backing.
session 3 (2 hours)	coordinator and up to 8 others	Mark if necessary. Layer, baste, and put the quilt into a frame. Begin quilting, using a simple quilting pattern.
session 4, 5, & 6 (2 hours each)	6 people	Continue hand quilting.
after session 6	1–2 people	Bind the quilt. Attach a label and casing.
after the quilt is finished	everyone	Hang the quilt for viewing. Invite everyone to celebrate work well done.

COOPERATIVE QUILTS MADE BY A CLASS

During the 1970s, Roberta Horton decided to make cooperative quilts with her intermediate-level adult education classes in California. Her goals were to have her students learn to quilt at a large frame, to learn more about color and design, and to gain confidence in quiltmaking by creating a quilt in 10 weeks. Since then, her classes have produced more than 40 quilts, each designed around a theme chosen at the first meeting.

Roberta's system is fast, and in order to finish the quilts on time each person must attend all the classes. To encourage attendance, each student puts her name tag into a box at the end of each session. At the final class, the name of the new owner is drawn, so regular attendance increases the chance of winning. Roberta's system varies somewhat from group to group, but the following is a typical schedule:

Week	Activity
1	Discuss possible themes. Choose one.
2, 3	Teacher purchases fabric and brings it to class. Students bring in design ideas, books, pictures, and so on. Designs are selected, drawn, and enlarged. Blocks are begun.
4	Blocks are due. Decide on a set. True the blocks to a uniform size. Sew the top together with sashes.
5	Layer, baste, and place the quilt in a large frame. Begin quilting.
6, 7, 8, 9	Each person quilts her own block, and contributes to the general quilting.
10	Finish quilting. Remove the quilt from the frame and sew the border. Draw the winner.

These classes are usually attended by 15 to 20 people. With Roberta's help, each student creates her own design, which is brought to the third class and cut out in fabric, but not sewn. The blocks are laid out to examine for necessary changes before actual sewing takes place. Unity of scale and design are achieved when each student can see everyone else's work and how her own relates to the whole.

Roberta's students are instructed to make the design cover 12 inches of a 14-inch block. The actual blocks are cut to measure 15 inches to allow for the shrinkage that often occurs when sewing stitches pull the block smaller. Later, the blocks are trued to 14½ inches, and sewn with ¼-inch seams so they finish to 14 inches. Roberta's favorite technique is appliqué, which she feels lends itself more easily to a theme than does patchwork. Evidence of this can be seen in the Pueblo Indian Designs Quilt (see C-24 in color section) made by one of her classes.

QUILTS BY MAIL

Many cooperative quilts have been made by mail. Because of the constraints imposed by distance, the coordinator of such a quilt often takes on decisions and tasks usually spread among the group members: design, buying the fabric, writing directions, cracking the deadline whip, sewing the blocks together, and writing volumes of correspondence. Although the coordinator need not actually perform all these tasks herself, she will have to initiate most of them and be responsible for seeing them through. The ideal situation is to have two or three neighbors share the job of coordinating a quilt made by mail.

Quilting can be done by one person with lots of time (and love), or by a core group of nearby contributors. The Teachers' Centers Quilt (see C-20 in color section) was assembled by ten contributors from all over New England who came to a two-day quilting and slumber party. They quilted half the blocks in 36 hours and had an especially memorable time doing it. You may be able to enlist the aid of your local quilt guild to help with the quilting.

By-mail quilts occasionally will attract the interest of people who at first said they wouldn't participate. Include these latecomers by asking them to make the label or compile a special notebook for the correspondence to present along with the quilt.

There are a few special design considerations for quilts made by mail. Individual appliqué blocks are a good choice for long-distance quilts. They allow for a direct, personal statement to be made that makes up for the lack of fellowship usually achieved through group meetings. Needleworkers accustomed to the greater investment of making an entire quilt are often seized by an urge to pour their usual amount of work into this single block, and incredible 12-inch masterpieces often result.

Very carefully thought out, clearly worded directions are essential for successful long-distance quilts, and it helps to explain the reasons behind requests. Sending out a background block is the only way to ensure the return of more or less equal-size blocks. Mark for the top on each one to keep the grain direction the same, and mark a very generous (one inch on each side) seam allowance with erasable pencil. Ask contributors to wash and iron their finished blocks before mailing them back. The blocks can easily be trued later by re-marking a uniform seam allowance, but this will leave the problem of correcting for fabrics that run, fray, or shrink to those who selected them. One good (though expensive) idea is to send out fabric swatches with each block. This may be the only hope for unifying the inevitable hodgepodge of colors and patterns that will emerge from such widely diverse scrapbags. Urge colorful, allover designs to avoid getting a great many outline "drawings" with much of the background fabric showing. A final design consideration is to think of a contingency plan for too many or too few blocks. With a by-mail quilt, one can never determine ahead of time how many will be returned.

Quilts made by mail cost more than others because of postage, photocopying, and photography costs. One solution is to invite each participant to send several stamped, self-addressed envelopes as well as a contribution to cover her share of the fabric, photocopying, and photography.

When the quilt is complete, hold a party for whomever is nearby, and take pictures. Then send a color print of the piece and an account of the festivities along with a thank-you note to everyone who contributed to the quilt.

I don't know whether anyone else has had the bonus that I have experienced. I have had notes from people I don't know! My cousins all live in the Midwest or on the East Coast, and I haven't seen most of them since I was a child, probably 20 years ago. I've never met any of their spouses. But here came warm, enthusiastic letters and lovely blocks from wives of these cousins. Also, touching letters from my elderly aunts saying, "I no longer can do any handwork because my arthritis is so bad, but I pieced this crazy-quilt patch on the sewing machine." This is truly a quilt of love and respect.

Kathy Huneke, San Leandro, California

TIME-SHARE QUILTS

If a collection of people (ideally, 6 to 12) agree to help make quilts for each other, they have become a time-sharing group. Each individual member in turn designs a quilt, buys fabric, cuts out the blocks, and provides instructions. The group sews the blocks, helps to seam the blocks together, bastes, and quilts. There are many variations to this basic plan.

Twelve members of the Quilters Guild of Greater Kansas City decided to piece quilts for each other.

We met once a month in members' homes. The hostess designed and cut out a quilt of her choice. Then the blocks were passed out to the other members of the group, who pieced them and returned them to their owner at the next meeting, at which time we received a new block. In this manner, each of us had at least 12 blocks for a quilt top. It was left to the owner to make enough more blocks to finish the top and put it together and quilt it.

Rosie Grinstead, Mission Hills, Kansas

Different types of quilts will appeal to various group members, and each person will have an opportunity to work on blocks she might not have chosen for herself. Working as a group presents dozens of opportunities for learning about design and color as well as about human nature. Again, Rosie Grinstead reports:

Before I distributed my blocks, I laid out each one on a large sheet of paper and pinned it in place. I also furnished a drawing of the finished layout, but even then one of the blocks came back with the center incorrectly made. Unfortunately, I didn't notice it until I was ready to baste the quilt together. I thought about leaving it, but finally decided to reconstruct the block. I told the group what had happened, but didn't mention who was responsible. The ironic part was that later I made an error on someone else's quilt. I still haven't lived that one down!

Betsy Tuttle, a Wisconsin artist, told us about an interesting variation of time-sharing that she and 11 other artists worked out. They chose a "night and day" theme, and each artist made 12 "night" blocks and 12 "day" blocks. Then they traded with the other group members. Eventually, each artist had 24 blocks, two each from 11 friends and two of his or her own. Some of the artists chose to sew their squares together quite traditionally, but the show, entitled "The 25th Square," held at the University of Wisconsin, also contained a quilted doghouse (trimmed with fur!) and a flying carpet or two. One of those original time-sharing artists, Annie Soerensen, subsequently moved to Denver, where she has kept alive the cooperative-quilt concept by engaging friends from her car pool in "earth and sky" quilts, with a weekly Sunday brunch to share their work in progress.

Wyn Reddall of Santa Rosa writes to describe her California guild's elaborate quilt-banking system:

Group quilts are almost a trademark of our Santa Rosa guild, which has developed its own methods and regulations for its quilt block program. It works like this: A person whose name is drawn is entitled to 20 blocks made according to her personal choice of design, color, and size. This winner makes up a set of 20 kits and passes these out to 20 participating members who complete the blocks and return them within a month. A record is kept, just like a bank account, by a yearly appointed activities chairperson, showing which blocks each member has made. If one's name is drawn to receive 20 blocks, one must repay the same number of blocks into the bank. If, when a name is drawn, that person already has 5 or 10 blocks on account, she need only make up the difference. Some members like to make blocks for 20 others first, so that when their name is drawn they don't owe the bank any blocks. Everyone needs 5 or 10 blocks on account to be eligible for her name to be drawn. About 9 or 10 sets of blocks are made every year, so that by now our guild has made over 50 sets, with very few repetitions in color or pattern. Perhaps half of these 50 already have been made into finished quilts.

Judy Robbins and the coauthors of *Not Just Another Quilt* devised a variation on time-sharing when they made a baby quilt for their editor's first child. Sarah Gobes designed and machine pieced the top, then passed it along to Mickey Lawler and Sheila Meyer for basting and hand quilting. Finally, Judy bound and mailed it. This process enabled them to divide the work on a small quilt and complete it quickly.

The Five Easy Piecers of Berkeley, California, have been making time-share quilts for years. They meet every Monday from 10 A.M. until their children come home from school, working on one quilt at a time. Each member is given two months, or eight Mondays, of work to be spent on any aspect of a quilt of her choice. Usually, the owner designs a quilt, buys and cuts the material, and distributes the blocks. The blocks are sewn at home between meetings, but the rest of the group contributes to the quiltmaking process. Often, a quilt will be finished in the two-month period, but if the project is large, the owner will either finish the remainder of the work herself or else wait until her two months comes around again. Mabry Benson's House Quilt (see C-5 in color section) was made by this method.

Tips for Cooperative Quiltmaking

Experienced quiltmakers from all over the United States have contributed to the following potpourri of design and construction tips, bound to be helpful in a cooperative project.

◆ For every 12 blocks, assign an extra block; that's about the ratio you need to get enough good, usable blocks.

◆ Buy the best fabric you can afford; ours frayed while we worked on it.

◆ We selected fabrics for our quilt by borrowing and trading with each other; it seemed someone else always had the right fabric for your block.

◆ Use only cotton on appliqués; dramatic materials proved too difficult for us to handle.

◆ The days of cotton that tears with the grain are gone. Measure carefully, and cut your fabric with scissors.

◆ A ½-inch seam allowance works better with our group than does the traditional ¼-inch.

◆ Buy sashing and backing material before the squares are made so you can work some of this into some of the blocks. Buy extra!

◆ We prewashed all our fabric with vinegar and water. This removes the sizing and leaves the fabric soft and easy to handle.

◆ Using a rotary blade cutter allowed us to cut out our sashes and borders in record time.

◆ We marked our future seam-lines in red transfer pencil. Later on, the red lines washed right out with baby shampoo.

◆ Inexperienced quilters will often resort to the "stab" method of quilting, which tends to produce nice-looking stitches on the top and a zigzag labyrinth on the reverse side. Someone should check the back of the quilt frequently to see how things look under there.

◆ From Jane Smith's direction sheet to her Maine group: "Do your best work. Use small, even stitches, and good-quality fabric and thread. Take pride in your work; you are embroidering your name on the block. This quilt is going to be around for a long time, and it would be a shame if your work was shoddy or your husband's old pj's wore out first."

◆ The quilt was put in a frame for the annual meeting, and everyone was invited to do some quilting during the convention.

◆ Some old quilts were started by one person who made a block and passed it along to another who would add a second block, and so on until the quilt top was finished. Then all the people who had made blocks got together and quilted it.

◆ We charge everybody one 12-inch pieced block as admission to our guild meetings. These are used as a door prize for the evening. It's a good way to try out new or unusual patterns.

◆ Press your quilt top gently. Don't stretch the fabric. Let the weight of the iron do the work.

◆ Bright colors photograph better than do subtle colors.

◆ We made a quilt top in our class and offered to tie it for the winner, or leave it for her to hand quilt later if she chose.

◆ Our group made a basket quilt. Each person filled her basket with whatever she chose—flowers, wine, fruit and bread, and so on.

◆ Our group made a sampler quilt. Each person chose her own 12-inch block and made copies of the pattern templates for all the others in the group.

◆ Everyone in our group gets one chance to win the quilt for every square she completes. Also, everyone receives one chance to win for every two hours of work she contributes.

◆ Everyone who worked on our quilt received a photocopy of the quilt, a short history, and a list of people who worked on it.

◆ The winner of our quilt held an open house for the women who made it.

♦　We devised a heavy clear-plastic cover to sandwich the quilt, and hung it all from a heavy pole. This way, people could see it but not touch it.

♦　We designed a freestanding Plexiglas shield to place in front of our quilt for display.

♦　At our quilt show, volunteers wearing white cotton gloves lift the quilts so passersby can see the back sides.

♦　Our group meets monthly for a combination of quilt sharing and food sharing. First brunch, then our quilt meeting; it seems like a nice combination to us.

Finishing Touches

SIGNING YOUR WORK AND MAKING A LABEL

The title of Mirra Bank's book, *Anonymous Was a Woman,* brought home to all of us the implications of failing to sign our works of art. We spend thousands of hours making quilts, wallhangings, pieced clothing, and the like, sewing with loving care because we'd like it to last 50 or 100 years or more, but we hesitate to sew on our name, the date, and something about ourselves. Everyone who owns an antique quilt has wondered about the person who made it. Eli Leon, a quilt collector in Oakland, California, who is especially interested in quilts made by black women, wanted to see how much he could learn about the people who signed one quilt he owns.

This very beautiful Duck Paddle Quilt from upstate New York has 42 signatures but no date, location, or presentation label. A few unusual names helped me locate the quilters in Baldwinville, New York, from the 1880 census lists. Because the quiltmakers were mostly in their late teens and early twenties, the quilt very likely was made for another young woman on the occasion of her marriage in 1878. One day, health permitting, I hope to make a trip to New York to find out, by examining church and town records, whether the women came together through a church or school, and eventually learn for whom the quilt was originally made. Perhaps I can find descendants of some of these women, who might lead me to photographs and additional information. At any rate, I thought I'd let you know about this group effort made in 1878, and how important it is for group quilts to be signed by their makers.

Quilts made of separate blocks are easily signed. The names can be prominent, or disguised within the design or piecing, adding the interest of a treasure hunt to the pleasure of viewing the quilt. The Great Things About Pittsburgh Quilt (see C-8 in color section) has embroidered on it the names of Pittsburgh's 78 neighborhoods between the curved quilting lines on the sashing. Another project could use this same idea for the quilters' signatures. In another instance, quilters' names appear in a large circle on the back of the Granville (Massachusetts) Bicentennial Quilt, and the makers of the Our Valley Quilt have worked their names among the vegetables and flowers of the title and signature block (figure 130). Whatever the system, if there are contributors who ignore the request to sign their work, a coordinator need have no hesitation about adding it for them, so long as there is no detraction from the visual impact of their work. Signatures are especially important when the receiver is a friend who will appreciate having this information right on the quilt in later years. An alternative to actually signing the quilt itself is to type a list of people who worked on the quilt and implore the owner to keep it with the piece.

There may be times when it is not appropriate to list all the separate names:

We resisted the idea of listing all the quilters' and embroiderers' names. Since it was to be a gift from all the women of the church, we thought this would be best accomplished by presenting it from the group as a whole. As it was, 125 women did work on it, probably more—there were so many drop-ins, we lost count.

Jackie Dodson, La Grange Park, Illinois

On the other hand, the entire reverse side of the 10-by-12-foot Boone Bicentennial Sampler (figure 131) is covered with 1,026 2-by-8-inch sponsor patches, each decorated by an individual, family, business, club, or charitable group. In this tiny space

130 (right). Our Valley;
title and signature block.

131 (below). Reverse side of the
Boone Bicentennial Sampler.

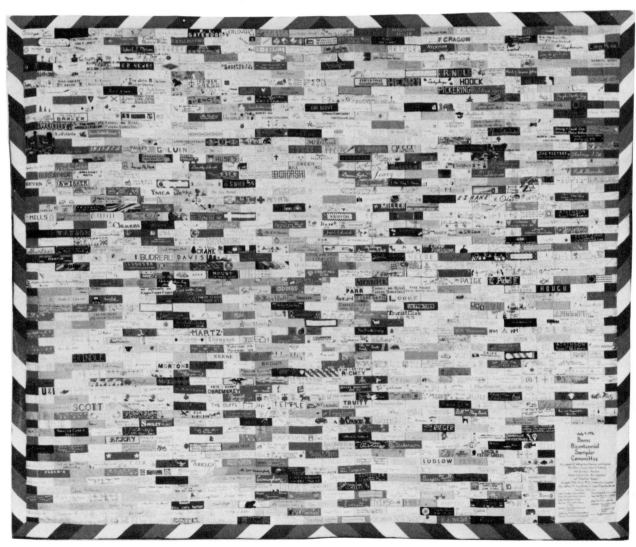

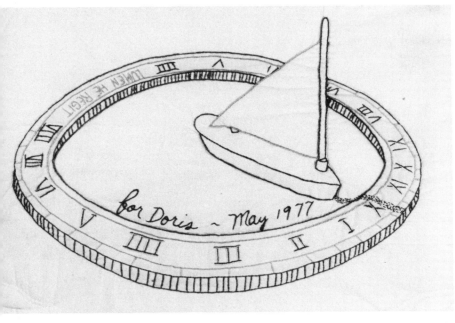

132 (upper left). Herb Society Quilt;
Herb Society of America
seal and logo block.

133 (upper right). Teachers' Centers Quilt;
Teachers' Centers Exchange logo block.

134 (lower left). Doris Kampe Friendship Quilt;
Sundial presentation block.

135 (lower right). Bunce Family Anniversary
Quilt; label block.

people managed to picture their homes, themselves, even something of their family history, with wonderful imagination and skill. Following an old tradition, each signer contributed one dollar to finance the project. From Ohio, Mary Potts Montgomery writes of the compromise that settled the question of signature for the makers of the Oberlin Quilt:

After much discussion, some felt it was historically valuable to sign the squares, but others thought it would detract from the overall design. As a compromise, the title and artist's signature were embroidered in red on the red sashing below each block. Only close observers can see them.

Signatures are one thing, labels another. Although Eli Leon managed to trace the makers of his quilt through their signatures, the absence of a label makes it difficult to ascertain for certain the original purpose of the quilt or the name of the recipient. A quilt label tells the quilt's purpose, the recipient's name, the place and date, and any words or symbols that may convey the spirit in which it was made and given. A group's logo may double as a label block, as it does for the Herb Society Quilt and the Teachers' Centers Quilt, figures 132 and 133. (The Onion block of the Herb Society Quilt, pictured in figure 132, is the logo of the Northern Illinois unit of the Herb Society of America. The Indian word for onion is "Chicago"—hence, the Chicago Skyline.) More formal label blocks, sometimes called presentation or dedication blocks, can be seen in figures 134 and 135 from the Doris Kampe Friendship Quilt and the Bunce Family Anniversary Quilt, respectively.

We believe that *all* quilts—and wallhangings and quilted clothing—deserve a label. Too many people sent us treasured photographs of quilts they had made and raffled, sadly adding, "We have lost track of this quilt and no longer know who owns it." If someone had embroidered the winner's name onto the quilt, she would probably remember it.

KEEPING TRACK OF YOUR QUILT

We know a family that recently found three quilts in their grandmother's attic after she died. They recognize the materials as those she used for other projects, but until the discovery none of them had ever seen the quilts themselves, and consequently have no idea when or why she was moved to make them. Where will your group quilt be 2 years, 10 years, 100 years from now? Will future owners know

its story? There are two ways to make sure they will, both equally important: first, by labeling the quilt; second, by documenting its making, giving one copy of the records to the owner and keeping another. Record keeping will include naming and photographing the quilt before it is given or awarded to its owner. In addition to helping the owner learn the quilt's history, the designers and makers of the quilt need to know its whereabouts. It is entirely appropriate to ask the new owners where they imagine the quilt will be in 5, 10, and 50 years. If they receive documents relating to how the quilt was made, they will be more likely to remember to keep you informed as to its location and owners.

DOCUMENTING YOUR QUILT

It should be a simple matter to keep a journal or scrapbook while making a quilt. There are a few key ingredients: the official name of the quilt; a list of contributors and what each one did; a description of the group and something of its history; a paragraph or two written after each stage is complete; and photographs taken as the quilt develops and after it is finished. The photographs should each be clearly identified on the backs (unlike those lying unlabeled in our own photo drawers).

If coordinating a quilt by mail, the documentation is easy. Simply make carbons or copies of the letters sent out and save all the replies in a folder. When the quilt is composed of separate squares, it is important to make a pictorial key with the subject and maker's name for each section to accompany your photographs of the makers and of the quilt.

We asked each person contributing to our parents' golden-anniversary quilt to include a postcard telling the story of their block. We plan to make individual photos of each block to put in a scrapbook along with the cards.

Jill Babinger, Syracuse, New York

Whoever volunteers to be the group's recorder should have license to inject her own personality into the process, making the documents an expression of herself and the group, as well as a historical record. Many groups contain a person ideally suited for the job, as is Dorothy Patrick Harris of the Summer Hill Quilters. Dorothy is unable to quilt many months out of the year because of a chronically painful injury, but she remains a vitally active contributor to the group—which meets at her house— through the very lively correspondence and record keeping she maintains as the resident historian. It is possible to organize the documentation so that everyone is drawn into reflecting upon the work (for instance, by interviewing each other in pairs, or by periodically tape-recording people's memories, feelings, and changing attitudes about their work).

There is much to be learned from groups that have taken the time, gathered the resources, and raised the funds to publish the records they have compiled. The following ideas are drawn from pamphlets published by the collaborators on the Chester (New York) Historical Quilt, the Onondaga County (New York) Bicentennial Quilt, and the Boone Bicentennial Sampler. (Consult the Resources section for information on how to obtain copies of these pamphlets.) The booklets suggested include the following:

♦ the official name of the quilt and of the group(s) involved in making it;
♦ a "key" to each block: the subject and the name of the maker;
♦ a photograph of the finished quilt;
♦ a separate photograph of the quilters themselves;
♦ a lively chronicle of the making of the quilt;
♦ a description of each block, including related historical information and stories;
♦ a brief biography/descriptive paragraph of each needleworker and historian;
♦ the names of all the dignitaries and historical figures whose names are stitched on the quilt;
♦ a list of books about the history of the area;
♦ acknowledgments and thank-yous.

In 1982, the Quilters of the Hudson Highlands (Newburgh, New York) undertook a winter project to refine their appliqué technique and to experiment with quilt-as-you-go construction. Working in neighborhood groups, they appliquéd traditional rose patterns, and when their quilt was complete they took the next step of making a booklet that gives the story of the quilt, a color photograph, instructions, and patterns for each of the designs and the layout.

Your record keeping need not be so extensive or formal. There may be only one aspect you wish to record. For the Teachers' Centers Quilt we simply kept a copy of all the correspondence. The women of the First Presbyterian Church in Columbia, Missouri, on the other hand, wrote a three-page description of the significance of the religious symbols in their Christian Symbols Quilt. These explana-

tions deepen the meaning of the quilt for both casual viewers and Religious Education students. And then there are those responsible for the Louisiana Extension Homemakers Council bicentennial quilt, on display at the Louisiana Museum of Natural History and Art, who put together another sort of presentation:

A set of slides showed each individual block, as well as the quilt, in its various stages. These slides, with the accompanying narrative, have been used by many homemaker councils to study Louisiana—its land, its people, and its places.
Betty Wood, Baton Rouge, Louisiana

Careful documentation can enhance the value of your quilt, which may be especially significant if you are planning to sell it to the highest bidder. The Dayton (Washington) Historical Depot Society members spent as much time researching the history of each house as they did embroidering its picture. The documents they produced were copied for the local library, the historical society, and the quilt's buyers. In another instance, purchasers of the Celebrity Signature Quilt (see C-13 in color section) wrote to thank the celebrities who had contributed their signatures, and received many letters in reply. Although it was not their original motivation for writing, these letters continue to increase the value of the quilt as time passes.

Creating historical records may have the side benefit of forcing you to be better organized:

I kept *all* the correspondence and articles having to do with the quilt. I started a three-by-five card for each person who contacted me and recorded on it all the additional information I might need later. This was invaluable for keeping track of the more than 500 people who eventually replied to my request that they contribute squares to a 50 States Quilt.
Charlene Anderson-Shea, Kaneohe, Hawaii

Another of the unforeseen rewards may be the sharing of local lore:

The assembled quilters worked to make their appliqué blocks as historically accurate as possible. Old photographs and books had been of help, but the greatest advantage—and enjoyment—were the recollections of some of the community's oldest residents, including octogenarian Rose Laroe, who related stories of what Chester had

been like when she was a girl and her grandfather owned the Washington Hotel on Main Street.
Patricia Edwards Clyne, Chester, New York

The makers of the Cambridge Women's Quilt (see C-11 in color section) recorded, edited, and published oral histories of all the people who worked on the project. In so doing, they found themselves documenting the lives of people whose stories are least recorded in traditional history sources, and came to appreciate all the more the richness of individual cultural traditions. For one participant, Nancy Kerr of Brighton, Massachusetts, making the quilt was a little like cooking. "You take all these separate ingredients, and you put them together, and when it's done it's like taking a quilt out of the oven. All of a sudden there's this *quilt,* that has all these colors and shapes in it. You see it evolve piece by piece, stir it up, and put it on the bed."

PHOTOGRAPHING THE QUILT

Photographs can help sell a quilt and will also enable the finished product to be shared with people who live far away. Extremely useful for publicity, documentation, and insurance records, they are absolutely mandatory if the quilt is to be entered in a show, a contest, or eventually be pictured in a publication. Textile photography is a challenge even for professional photographers. We are not expert quilt photographers, but out of necessity have become good at it, and you can, too.

SAY "CHEESE"
Although a bed is the logical setting for most quilts, amateur photographers would do well to avoid the three-dimensional and perspective problems inherent in photographing bedcovers. A quilt can be photographed to its best advantage while hung flat against a white or neutral-colored wall. Stand *directly* in front of it, using a tripod if at all possible. Position the camera so that the center of the lens focuses exactly on the center of the quilt. Frame the quilt in the lens so that the image fills almost to the edges of the viewfinder, but leave some space around the image on all sides because a bit of the edge will be lost when the film is processed. Be *sure* all the edges of the camera are parallel to the wall. If you tilt the camera up, down, left, or right, the image will also tilt, and the quilt will look like a trapezoid instead of a rectangle. Many such trapezoidal quilts have been created by photographers at

136. Photographing quilts and quiltmakers at the Cambridge Women's Quilt Project.

quilt shows who were unable to stand squarely in front of their subject.

In addition to a full shot of the entire quilt, it is desirable to come as close as equipment will allow to take some detail shots. These close-ups, filling the lens with interesting areas of the quilt, are meant to show stitching as well as design. Consider what will show around the edges of these details before pressing the shutter.

OUTDOOR VS. INDOOR PHOTOGRAPHY
Amateur photographers get their best quilt pictures outdoors, because that's where the best light is, enabling the colors to be reproduced most accurately. Massachusetts quilt artist Nancy Halpern photographs her quilts hanging on the side of an old barn. The rustic barn-boards are easy to pin into, and the

wood that shows around the quilt's perimeter blends attractively with the fabric.

Outdoor photography should take place on a cloudy-bright day. Direct sunlight creates too much contrast on the surface of the fabric, causing unflattering shadows and highlights. The cloudy-bright conditions are perfect for illuminating the quilt evenly, showing up the textural effect created by the quilting stitches. Unfortunately, while outdoors one is at the mercy of the elements. Wind, rain, and direct sun can ruin your chances of getting a good photograph of a beautiful quilt. And when working against a deadline, it can be nerve-racking to wait for the weather to cooperate.

Indoor photography allows you to control conditions, but the trade-off is that the light is never as good as it is outdoors, and so the color may suffer, particularly if the quilt contains a wide range of them.

Most flash attachments are incapable of illuminating the large surface area of a quilt evenly. A "hot spot" or lighter area will appear in the center of the quilt, and the sides will be dark by comparison. We have had good luck using an automatic flash attachment supplemented by two daylight-balanced floodlights directed toward the sides of the quilt. Nevertheless, no matter how good a flash arrangement may be, it is the nature of flash photography to wash out the texture of the quilting stitches; because both the indented rows of quilting and the unquilted areas are equally illuminated, the quilt is made to appear flat, with no quilting stitches showing. If it is desirable for the quilting to show, take outdoor photographs or use four floodlights, placing one pair to the side of your quilt, to highlight the bas-relief effect.

SLIDES VS. COLOR PRINTS VS. BLACK-AND-WHITE

If the quilt is entered in a quilt show or contest or submitted for publication, reproducible quality slides will be requested. Take both full shots and details, and enter only the best slides. Good slides do not necessarily convert to good color prints, even when processed by a custom photography lab. We prefer to use slide film for slides and print film for color prints. Film quality varies a great deal, and processing varies even more. We suggest you use only Kodak film, and Kodak processing, too, unless a local custom lab has proven trustworthy.

Black-and-white pictures are often handy to have, especially for newspapers, but one need not shoot in black-and-white. Both color transparencies (slides) and color negatives can be converted to black-and-white prints. We have this work done by a local custom black-and-white lab. These color conversions, however, are more expensive than shooting in black and white in the first place, and they are never quite as crisp and clear. Two cameras, one loaded with color slide film and the other with black-and-white film, will speed the picture-taking process. See Michael James's *Quiltmaker's Handbook II* and Robbie and Tony Fanning's *Complete Book of Machine Quilting* for additional comments on this subject.

CELEBRATIONS AND ACKNOWLEDGMENTS

If the group has enjoyed making a quilt together and the members have grown close and begun to appreciate each other in new ways, it will be important for them to hold a special celebration when the quilt is finished. A celebration acknowledges all the hard work and creativity, values the friendships that have formed, marks the end of work on the quilt, and eases the passing of the quilt to its new owner. Everyone will benefit if this occasion is planned for, if photographs are taken, if all the participants are present, and if there is a bit of celebratory ritual—humorous as well as serious—that marks the making of this quilt as an important accomplishment in everyone's lives.

Groups that make four or five quilts each year and know they will continue to quilt together may simply spend half an hour taking pictures, eating something special, and reflecting together about the quilt—what they learned from it and how they feel about it—before moving on to making the next one. Groups that gathered expressly to make one quilt need a more elaborate occasion because they are dealing not only with giving up the quilt but also with ending their group gatherings. Even when quilts have been made by a widely dispersed group and coordinated by mail, it is important to create a sense of completion and celebration through a photograph and a thoughtful letter that includes an account of the presentation to the new owner, like the letter at the end of chapter 1 that Barbara Wysocki wrote her family after delivering Nanny's Album Quilt.

These celebrations also provide a time to say thank you to all the people who helped create the quilt. As mentioned before, this should not be left to the coordinator to organize, since she is often the person the rest of the group most want to thank. One coordinator was surprised by being taken to dinner as thanks for her work and for all the time the members had spent at her home.

Gladys Boalt of Patterson, New York, writes of how her group celebrated the first hanging of the Putnam County Quilt:

> When we finished the quilt, we had a reception for everyone who had worked on it, including the newspaper people who had given us lots of advice about local history. We also invited people who had been directly involved in what went *on* the quilt, like one elderly gentleman who was pictured on one of the blocks. Then we gave out corsages to all the quilters.

PRESENTATIONS

Once the making of the quilt has been celebrated, it is time to plan its presentation to the new owner(s). In most cases, the quilt will not be going to complete strangers, and even if it is, the recipients will recognize the history and care with which it was made. Still, it is true that only people who have made a quilt truly appreciate what goes into it. Use your presentation to help the owner learn about quilting, if that is appropriate, by including a simple quilting demonstration. Present the documents you have kept; instruct in the care, cleaning, and hanging of the quilt. Request to be kept up to date on the quilt's location, ask about its possibly being lent back for display, and raise the question of how it will be used—obliquely conveying the message that you agree with Erma Bombeck, who has written that if anyone approached one of her quilts with a pair of scissors she would see that they were arrested for assault with a deadly weapon.

These two descriptions of presentations may inspire further ideas for other groups. They certainly leave one with the feeling that in each case the treasured quilt was dispatched with love, care, and appropriate ceremony.

Giving a party with a quilt as guest of honor may strike some as strange, but the Friends of the Library felt their quilt—and the quilters—deserved such recognition. Therefore, the public was invited to an afternoon social at the Chester Town Hall, where the volunteers were formally thanked. The highlight of the party was a slide show detailing the progress of the quilt from the first planning session in January to the presentation in June. Even more impressive, however, was the solid round of applause given the quilters as they were introduced and thanked for their contribution to the community.

Patricia Edwards Clyne, Chester, New York

When the planning committee for the 1977 national conference of the American Crafts Council asked me to design and partially complete a presentation quilt for ACC's founder, Aileen Osborn Webb, to be completed and given to her at the conference, I chose to make a whole cloth quilt in white with cream-colored borders. On each side were large quilted letters that spelled out her name and the council's; at the corners were quilted craftsmen's hands and tools.

The quilt was put in a frame at the conference, and 25 well-known artist-craftspeople were invited to draw a motif of their work on the quilt. Quilters and stitchers—men and women alike—rallied around to complete the work during the week, finishing fifteen minutes before the presentation dinner. And how glorious that presentation was! After a day of group projects in clay, wood and fiber—all in celebration of Mrs. Webb's devotion to the crafts—was a picnic supper on the lawn with several hundred ACC craftspeople, in appropriately arty dress. A few different presentations were made, but the quilt seemed to be the most personal and appreciated.

Bets Ramsey, Chattanooga, Tennessee

LETTING GO OF YOUR COOPERATIVE QUILT

It is natural and inevitable for the creators of a quilt to feel it belongs to them. It is their creation, both in idea and tangible actuality. The moment of transfer from the group to the new owner is a turning point in the life of the quilt—one that should be a high point of celebration, satisfaction, and pride, but is too often a low point of discouragement or resentment.

When it was time for our Ranch and Cattle Brands Quilt to gain a new owner, we were all nearly moved to tears. It was like losing a friend. But soon our sadness changed to fury. The person who won it wanted to sell it to acquire a deposit for a new piano! Fortunately for everyone, the

Whitehead Memorial Museum purchased it from her, and now it rests appropriately a few yards away from the gravestone that reads "Judge Roy Bean: Law West of the Pecos."

Charlotte Ayer Salinas, Del Rio, Texas

Because the historical society was attempting to raise money for preservation projects, they decided to raffle the quilt. The raffle brought $2,000, and the winner, a local pharmacist, displays the quilt for public view. Nevertheless, many members have come to regret the decision. No sooner were the final stitches applied than society members were asking, "Couldn't we keep this, after all?"

Geraldine Lawrence, Centralia, Washington

The first step in letting the quilt go is to truly "finish" the quilt—label it, photograph it, document its history, prepare it for hanging, and write up instructions for its care for the new owners. Then hold a celebration to mark the transition from the time the quilt was being made to the new period in which it will have new owners, taking the time to congratulate yourselves on a job well done and to share feelings of pride and loss.

There are three kinds of new owners for group-made quilts. How to plan for letting go of the quilt and passing it on to them will differ in each of the three situations.

When the plan from the beginning is to give the quilt to a specific individual who has been kept in mind throughout the process, the makers may have difficulty finishing the quilt—especially if the presentation is occasioned by a need to say farewell—but they will seldom have difficulty giving it up. Compare, for example, these two experiences of the Boise Peace Quilt Project:

As we worked on our first Peace Quilt we would picture the Soviet women to whom we were sending it. We talked a lot about them and were eager to finish the quilt and send it to them. Our second quilt had its rocky moments—partly, I think, because we didn't know until it was almost finished to whom it would be awarded. It's much better to be making a quilt for someone specific, rather than for an abstract receiver like our second quilt's "worthy winner of the Boise Peace Award.

Anne Hausrath, Boise, Idaho

The second kind of new owner occurs in groups that make a quilt together and then have a drawing among themselves to see who gets to keep it. If they have taken time to celebrate their work before the drawing, this practice seldom causes bad feelings among the group. Ideally, the members have a long-term commitment to making enough quilts for everyone eventually to win one. Some groups have a policy that winners cannot resubmit their names until everyone else has won one also. Larger groups for whom that would be impractical require winners to contribute to a certain number of subsequent quilts before their names go back into the hat. Other groups treat each quilt as a separate opportunity and put names in according to the amount of work each person has contributed, thus increasing the more active contributors' chances. Most quilting groups establish rules for how names are added to the pot that make these drawings scrupulously fair. And then there's always the solution arrived at by the makers of The Sun Sets on Sunbonnet Sue Quilt—they opted for joint ownership. The first year, each of the members "owned" it for a month.

The greatest problems with letting go of a group quilt occur with the third kind of new owner—the stranger who has won it in a raffle. Too often this is someone who knows little about quilting and therefore cannot appreciate the skill and hours of work that went into it. Even quilters themselves sometimes have been known to be guilty of rather callous attitudes toward work they did not do first hand.

A group can do several things to alleviate the disappointment and resentment naturally felt when a stranger or an unappreciative person wins a raffle quilt. The first is to focus as much on the purpose of the raffle—usually raising funds for an important cause everyone feels strongly about—as on the quilt itself. When raffle proceeds from the Eastern Long Island Quilter's Guild provided two scholarships for Southampton College fine arts students, they received many grateful thank-yous:

I would like to express my deepest appreciation for your generous award. This year I was shocked to find my financial aid had been cut to less than half, and at that point was forced to take a critical look at my education here at Southampton College. I felt I had received a great deal from the school and the art department, and decided to try to work out the financial situation. The news of your award was truly a blessing and could not

have come at a more needed time. Thank you for caring enough to assist art students here.
K. Fornof, Southampton, New York

Recognition and thanks of this kind certainly help alleviate any hesitation one may have had about letting go of a quilt. Moreover, recognition and thank-yous can actually be built in to a group's quilt-finishing celebration and into the presentation organized for passing the quilt on to its new owner. The presentation can be used to gain publicity for the group's cause—another way to focus on the quilt's fundraising aspects. The new owner can be given a pictorial key to the quilt with the addresses of the makers—implying that a thank-you letter is in order, as indeed it is.

Raffle tickets for the Herb Society Quilt were sold only among members of the society, which is one way to avoid the possibility that the quilt will go to someone outside the group. (A sad but ironic postscript is that the night after the winner was chosen, the quilt was stolen—probably by a stranger to both quilting and the Herb Society.)

But sometimes a stranger turns out to be the ideal winner:

Miriam Weber, who won our Scenes of San Francisco Quilt, owns a bed-and-breakfast place built in 1895 (figures 6 and 7). She has an appreciation of quilts and will display ours for her guests. We are always relieved and happy when our quilts find a good home.
Darlene Hartman, San Francisco, California

Last summer I took a trip to Alaska, a dream I've had for a long time. I visited many places and spent two nights in Fairbanks. In the hotel lobby I noticed a sign for a quilt show, and since my mother is a quilter, I decided to go. It was terrific, and I took lots of pictures, including one photo of a quilt that was being made at the show. On the way out I decided to take a chance on the quilt—actually two, one for Mom and one for me. Six weeks later I got a notice telling me that I had won it! It is beautiful, sampler style, made by the Cabin Fever Quilters of Fairbanks, Alaska. I love and treasure my group quilt.
Marian Meier, Glen Ellyn, Illinois

It may be that the difficulties groups have with finishing and giving up their cooperative quilts are not caused by their attachment to the quilts alone, but by their attachment to each other, which they do not want ended. There is no need to feel that giving up the quilt means giving up the fellowship. The obvious solution? Start to work on another one!

The holder of the lucky ticket will be taking away a real prize, and we'll be sorry to see it go. But those of us who worked on it are the winners, too. We won't have anything to carry home under our arms, but we'll have memories that will last us for a long, long time. Then—who knows—perhaps we'll make another.
Dorothy Sanborn, Bridgton, Maine

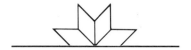

A Supplement for Fundraisers

Any quilt can be used to raise funds, but through the years groups of quilters have learned how to increase the value and appeal of these quilts, while at the same time decreasing the time it takes to produce them. More than a third of all the quilts pictured in *Hands All Around* were made as fundraisers.

SETTING GOALS

Setting goals for the monetary and the nonmonetary benefits of fundraising work is essential to the project's success. Clearly stated, the hopes that goals inspire quickly become expectations that give added life to the sometimes wearisome tasks of working against a deadline, selling tickets, stirring up the local media, and taking the quilt from place to place for display. But consider whether the time and work required to make and promote a successful raffle or auction quilt are worth the expected profit. One very experienced fundraiser told us that the groups she works with find they can raise $1,000 for each month of ticket sales. She believes raffling quilts is the most pleasant way to raise funds for an organization because it's fairly easy to find people to sell tickets and easier to get people to buy tickets. It's also a very good way to create an opportunity for otherwise busy people to do some quilting.

RAFFLES

Organizers and workers on a raffle must be highly committed to the cause for which the funds are being raised, for there is much work to be done. Many quilters may volunteer to make the quilt, but their primary commitment will be to the quilt itself. Unless they are also supportive of the fundraising cause, it would be a mistake to look to the *quilters* to organize the goal-setting, deadlines, permits, ticket printing and sales, displays, accounting, raffle, and presentation. One would do well to consider expanding the group to include others who support the cause but are not needleworkers to help with these parts of the fundraising. Good publicity and the resulting lucrative raffle ticket sales are part of the reward quilters get for their efforts. Morale can deteriorate rapidly if a beautiful quilt is produced and no one is able to promote it successfully.

Just as important as commitment is designing an attractive, durable quilt that will appeal to a wide variety of people and look nice in a number of settings. It is a good strategy to establish a reputation for making excellent quilts. If a raffle becomes a yearly event, and one's sales network remains in place, people may start coming *to you* seeking raffle tickets.

RAFFLE TICKET SALES

Successful fundraising with a raffle quilt ultimately depends upon how many tickets are sold. More tickets will be sold if the winner does not have to be present at the drawing. Many groups no longer number the individual tickets and stubs (unless required to do so by state law). Instead, they keep careful accounts of the number of tickets given to and collected from each salesperson and make sure the totals match, so that everyone who buys a ticket can be assured his or her stub is included in the drawing. Printed tickets and attractive photographs of the finished quilt convey a professional image, and a more professional raffle will have a wider appeal and a solid reputation.

The ticket must include certain information: the name of the quilt and the group that made it; the cause; any other sponsors; the date, time, and place of the drawing; whether or not the contributor must be present to win; and (if required by law) the ticket number. The stub need only have a place for the name, address, and telephone of the contributor, as well as the matching ticket number, if this applies. Accurate records must be kept, and all stubs carefully stored during the months before the raffle.

Almost all raffle tickets are sold for $1.00. Most groups also offer a discounted price that encourages a $5.00 donation (for example, six or seven tickets for $5.00).

Because the success of any fundraising depends upon the salesforce, it may pay to have a special "kickoff" and introduction to the quilt at the beginning of the ticket sales period. As an example, for our next church quilt-raffle we plan to hold a potluck dinner and quilt show-and-sharing evening, to which interested church members will bring a covered dish and their family quilts to be hung or placed on tables around the room. After dinner, two of the raffle quiltmakers will talk—no more than 10 minutes each—about the quilt and what making it has meant to them, with reactions and additions from the audience. Then *everyone* will go home with tickets to sell.

AUCTIONS

An excellent auctioneer is as important an ingredient to a successful auction as the quilt. The simplest way to find an auctioneer and to widely publicize your quilt is to auction the quilt at an occasion organized by others. An all-white trapunto quilt-as-you-go queen-size quilt that took 1,300 hours to make was the highlight of the 1983 Fort Wayne, Indiana, Philharmonic Orchestra Auction. The quilt that was made for the Iditarod Sled-Dog Race suffered as a fundraiser because its makers were so busy completing the piece that they did not have time to display it before the race or to plan well for its inclusion in the banquet where it was auctioned.

Many church groups are not comfortable with the element of chance involved in raffles, nor with the competitive bidding that is the essence of the auctioneer's art. These groups sell their quilts to the highest bidder through sealed bids. The Quilting Bee of the Grand Haven, Michigan, United Methodist Church of the Dunes makes many quilts that are sold in this way at their biennial bazaars. The proceeds are used to support missions, local concerns, and church needs. In other instances, the Mariner's Compass Quilt (figure 16) and the Celebrity Signature Quilt (C-13) were both sold by sealed bids (sometimes called "silent auction") to raise funds for their church groups.

Conducting one's own quilt auction is a large undertaking, but auctions can be a wonderful service to your community and may also result in abundant profits— *if* you supply a commensurate abundance of quilts. Following are several group-auction guidelines, gathered from various groups and one large auction in particular, chaired by Jeannine Hendrickson, of over 300 items (including 50 quilts) made by groups to raise funds for a permanent building for the Santa Clara Valley Quilt Associations's American Museum of Quilts and Related Arts.

◆   Have as wide a representation of quilt types as possible. When the donating quilter knows that her quilt will be the only one of its kind, she will take greater care to make it skillfully.
◆   Leave the patterns or construction methods that take the most time to large groups, who will also benefit from trying out new techniques or reaching new levels of skill.
◆   Arrange a heavily advertised public showing before the date of the auction.
◆   Do not schedule an auction until an experienced, dynamic auctioneer has been hired. Even if you are selling the quilts at a silent auction with sealed bids, the master of ceremonies for the event is a key to success.

DESIGNING A SUCCESSFUL FUNDRAISING QUILT

We have said a good deal about quilt design and the special considerations of designing with a group and for a cooperative project in chapter 2. Here are a few additional design ideas particularly appropriate for quilts that will be used to raise funds.

◆   Design and finish the quilt so that it will serve more than one purpose: the single bedcover (shown in C-4 in the color section) that can double as a wallhanging is an example. Quilters from Beatrice, Nebraska, designed one sampler quilt so that the edges of the blocks would fall attractively on a double, queen-, *or* king-size bed.
◆   Bright colors and strong graphic design are both assets, especially if the quilt is to appear in newspapers, on television, and in photographs carried by ticket sellers or on posters.
◆   One basic layout that adapts well to groups of quilters is an outside row of blocks surrounding a large central panel. The quilts Rainbow Fantasy (figure 9) and Flying Machines—Up, Up, and Away (figure 10) are good examples. The dynamic design of Flying Machines was the key factor in its raising $4,200 in PTA raffle ticket sales. The central panel can be very dramatic and display outstanding needlework, while participants with less time or skill can choose to make one of the smaller blocks.
◆   Outstanding, one-of-a-kind quilts and ones made by a group with a reputation for producing masterpieces of workmanship are guaranteed to raise more funds than

those without good design or with inadequate stitching. It takes more time to make a masterpiece, but for many groups the extra funds raised and the new skills learned compensate for the greater effort.

♦ Be sure the quilt is durable. This is an important selling feature.

SATISFYING THE RULES AND REGULATIONS

The very first step in planning an auction or raffle is to find out the local and state regulations for these activities. Many states have extremely strict requirements for the group sponsoring the fundraising, for the advertising and ticket sales, for collecting and dispersing funds, and for the way the event itself must be organized.

It may be necessary to be a nonprofit organization, and attaining nonprofit status can be a lengthy and complicated process. There will be benefits from having a tax-exempt status if more than $1,500 is raised. (This amount differs from state to state.) The Internal Revenue Service can answer questions about how to obtain this status, given a group's purposes and bylaws, can advise as to the kind of accounting required by nonprofit groups and can suggest which expenses may or may not be deductible. These are not necessarily quickly settled matters, so do not make the mistake of putting them at the bottom of your To Do list. Nevertheless, if obtaining nonprofit and/or tax-exempt status proves to be very complicated, it may be possible to jointly sponsor the raffle with another charitable group, service organization, church, or the like. You would then be responsible for making the quilt, while they would sponsor the raffle or auction.

We suggest that once you know what the regulations are, you spend a few hours contacting other groups in your area that have conducted raffles. At the same time, search out the lawyers who have helped groups similar to yours obtain nonprofit status and learn how they went about it. Be sure to take every opportunity to thank and give credit for any alliances and donations you benefit from.

Nonprofit groups must spend their funds to achieve their incorporated purposes, unless the funds have been specifically raised for a particular charitable cause. So be very clear from the beginning in all advertising about why the funds are being raised and exactly how they will be dispersed. It is also important to consider what will happen if a good deal more money is raised than was anticipated. Occasionally, a quilt show becomes the biggest event of the season. Barely Enough (figure 46) was one of three raffle quilts made by the East Bay Heritage Quilters for their well-attended quilt exhibit at Mills College. The quilters were surprised and delighted to find that many attending had contributed $3.00, instead of the expected $1.00, buying one ticket for each of the quilts. By the end of the exhibit the three quilts had earned an incredible $11,800.

DISPLAY

Wide and frequent display of a finished quilt will boost ticket sales or auction attendance. The link between displaying a quilt and selling tickets is an important key to a profitable raffle. It is wise to finish a raffle quilt many months before the raffle date, to make it easy to transport and hang and to arrange for frequent advance viewing accompanied by ticket sales—at shopping centers, churches, banks, museums, libraries, community and school events, quilters' gatherings, craft shows and fairs. A large, soft bag will keep the quilt clean as it's carried from place to place. Needless to say, the quilt should be clearly labeled and carefully watched while being displayed.

The women who made the Sanibel Quilt (C-15) hung it two days a week on the porch of a local store—one of the island's main gathering places—covered with a large sheet of protective plastic. They sold tickets to almost everyone who went through the door, and raised $4,700.

If you are running short on a deadline, it will probably be worth the effort to set up a quilting frame in several public places while the quilting is being finished. Another simple, inexpensive, and very effective way to "display" the quilt is to provide every ticket seller with an attractive color print of it to show prospective contributors. (But make sure your design and colors are ones that photograph well.)

We heard one disheartening story about a quilt that was inadvertently damaged while being displayed. An antique dealer had offered to hang the quilt top in a window that didn't get direct sun. In fewer than three weeks the quilt had faded—some colors worse than others, some fabrics worse than others. Green and blue fabrics have been known to fade under the fluorescent lights in stores. Fortunately, this group was able to salvage their quilt by replacing the badly faded pieces, but they could not have done so if it had already been quilted.

PUBLICITY

Local newspapers are probably the best advertising medium for publicizing a quilt and a cause. Try for coverage in a feature story. Ask the paper to send out a reporter; they may very well say no, but only because their reporters are busy with other things. All papers welcome human interest stories, and all quilts have the makings of an excellent human interest feature. So write and submit an article yourself, including at least one five-by-seven glossy black-and-white photograph.

Posters are easy to produce and are widely seen. An eye-catching poster that includes a color photograph of the quilt can do a great deal to boost ticket sales. The color and design of the poster should relate to the color and design of the quilt, so that people will associate the two.

Radio talk shows are a possiblity for telling about the

quilt. Be prepared with any amusing or touching stories about how the quilt was made. Television coverage is more difficult to arrange. Your best chances will be on local channels, particularly cable stations, that have interview shows or ones that feature local events.

Hold a publicity brainstorming session early in the making of your quilt. Can the project be tied in with an upcoming community event? Quilters in Claremont, California, did just this with their quilt that raised funds to send their boys' soccer team to England; they took advantage of the town's 75th birthday and chose a theme of historic buildings and places in town. The completed quilt was in demand at all the celebrations and in all the buildings.

OTHER WAYS TO USE QUILTS TO RAISE FUNDS

Nelly's Needlers of Mount Vernon, Virginia, take their name from Martha "Nelly" Washington, who was an expert needleworker. They raise funds for the Woodlawn Plantation, a national trust property, by making reproductions of special quilts in the Woodlawn collection. The Barclay Farmstead Quilters make custom quilts and contribute the profits to the Barclay Farmstead, a historic restoration in Cherry Hill, New Jersey. Many churches have quilting groups that quilt tops for customers on a waiting list that often extends up to two years. These quilt tops may be old or new—some people have found tops in their grandmother's attic or at a yard sale; other stitchers enjoy the challenge of putting together geo-metric shapes to create a pattern but do not enjoy or don't have the time for the more tedious task of actually quilting. Methods of charging vary; often it's by the spool of thread.

Several groups (the Bowers Museum, the California Marine Mammal Society, and many historical societies and service groups, for example) have used their quilts to promote their activities without selling the quilts. As a result of displaying the quilt they have received contributions, publicity, and other resources and services they otherwise would not have had. The Texture of Fabric—Texture of Life and Cambridge Women's Quilt were both the work of projects funded by federal, state, and city arts and humanities grants. We strongly encourage artists, needleworkers, and local quilt guilds to apply together to their state council on the arts, to federal sources, and to private foundations for funds to support cooperative quiltmaking projects.

Some groups have extended the fundraising power of especially beautiful or interesting quilts by selling postcards, notecards, patterns, brochures, documentary books, or posters of them. To do this you need a masterpiece quilt, a professional photographer who understands the special demands of photographing quilts, a sympathetic printer who charges reasonable rates for small-quantity jobs, up to $500 front money, and a sales and distribution plan. Quite a few of the quilts pictured in this book are available on postcards or posters, or are featured in historical or pattern booklets. The Resources Section contains information on all those that we have received.

Final Words

Annotated List of Illustrations

Each of the quilts pictured in this book is described in detail below. All drawings in the book are by Judy Robbins.

Color plate 1 *Hecht Wedding Quilt*
Made by seven friends of Barbara and Fred Hecht of Evanston, Illinois, as a wedding present. Coordinated by Mary Jo Deysach, Marion Huyck, Pam Osmand, Lee Burnham, Janet Bourguechon, and Betty Swanson. Designed by Ed Larson. Photo by Mary Jo Deysach.

Color plate 2 and figures 38 and 39 *Flowers of the Bible*
Made by the Lutheran Church Women of Grace Lutheran Church, La Grange Park, Illinois, as a wedding present for Dave and Carol Hedlin. Coordinated by Jackie Dodson and Joan Stone. Designed by Jackie Dodson (using drawings from *All the Plants of the Bible* by Winifred Walker, Doubleday, 1979). Photo by William S. Worline. Figure 38: Fir block made by Louise Pearson. Figure 39: Melon block made by Gloria Jackson. Photos 38 and 39 by Charles A. Dodson.

Color plate 3 *Ferndale Heritage Quilt*
Made by sixteen women of the Ferndale California Quilters as a fundraiser for a local museum. Coordinated by Virginia Jorgensen and Betty Genzoli. Photo by Richard Adams. Postcards available from Box 876, Ferndale, CA 95536.

Color plate 4 *Lote House Quilt*
Made by the Ladies of the Evening Quilt Club. Designed by Cynthia Biagiotti. Photo by Jerry Yorko. Complete directions and full-size patterns available from L.O.T.E.

Quilt Club, Box 456, Georgetown, CT 06829. Appeared in *Quilt* magazine, Fall 1981.

Color plate 5 *Houses*
Made by Five Easy Piecers, Berkeley, California, as a time-share project. Designed and owned by Mabry Benson. Photo by Gretchen Thomas.

Color plate 6 *Beyer Beware*
Made by the Weston, Massachusetts, Quilt Workshop. Photo by Nancy Halpern.

Color plate 7 *Putnam County Quilt*
Made by needlewomen of Putnam County, New York, as a 1976 bicentennial project. Designed and coordinated by Gladys Boalt. Photo by Marc Cohen.

Color plate 8 *The Great Things About Pittsburgh Quilt*
Made by contest entrants from Pittsburgh neighborhoods. Coordinated by Linda Eidinger and Sue Brophy. Blocks joined and quilted by Quilters Triangle. Owned by the City of Pittsburgh, Pennsylvania. Use coordinated by the Neighborhoods for Living Center of the Urban Redevelopment Authority, 515 Second Ave., Pittsburgh, PA 15219. Photo by Michael Friedlander. Postcards available from the Center.

Color plate 9 *Baltimore Culture and Heritage: Past, Present, and Future*
Made by the Summer Hill Quilters for a Baltimore quilt contest. Designed and coordinated by Phyllis Wilkinson. Property of the City of Baltimore, Maryland. Photo by Peter Liebhold. Appeared in *Better Homes and Gardens Remodeling Ideas*, Fall 1982, and *Country Home and*

Kitchen Ideas, Fall 1982. Copyrighted 1981 by the Summer Hill Quilters.

Color plate 10 *Washington Perspective*
An original design, hand-pieced and assembled by Anne Baker, Joan Dorman, Beatrice Fuller, Muriel Hanson, Dorothy Higbie, Judy Mahaffie, Betty Rath, Nicole Verdant, Mary Watson, with Mary Coyne Penders as coordinator, known as The Capitol Quilters. Photo by Paul Kennedy. A book by Mary Coyne Penders that describes, in part, the making of this quilt, is available from Quietwork Publications, 2600 Oak Valley Drive, Vienna, VA 22180. Copyrighted 1982 by The Capitol Quilters, all rights reserved.

Color plate 11 and figures 35, 49, and 136 *Cambridge Women's Quilt*
Made by women and girls in the Cambridge, Massachusetts, area working on a project sponsored by the Cambridge Arts Council. Cindy Cohen, Project Director; Pattie Chase and Susan Thompson, Quilt Coordinators. Postcards, exhibition brochure, and oral history excerpts available. See Resources for address and related publications and projects. Photo C-11 by Barry Cohen. Figure 35: Sara Bansen and her friend Lili work together on the Take Back the Night block. Figure 49: Terry Wright and Cindy Cohen consider the layout of the blocks. Figure 136: Bonnie Burt. Photos 35, 49, and 136 by Claudette Lecomte.

Color plate 12 and figure 104 *Shadows Quilt*
Made by 28 friends of Philomena Wiechec. Coordinated by Evelyn Anderson and Elizabeth Voris. Photos by Philomena Wiechec. Quilting pattern available from Santa Clara Valley Quilt Association, Box 792, Campbell, CA 95009. Other Celtic patterns available from Philomena Wiechec, Celtic Design Co., 19170 Portas Dr., Saratoga, CA 95070. Appeared in *Celtic Quilt Designs* by Philomena Wiechec, Saratoga, CA: Celtic Design Co., 1980.

Color plate 13 *Celebrity Signature Quilt*
Made by the Storrs, Connecticut, Congregational Church Quilters to raise funds for a new organ. Coordinated by Janet Aronson and Arlene Hewes. Owned by Alice P. Whitaker. Photo by Judy Robbins.

Color plate 14 *Appliqué Sampler*
Made by members of the Eastern Long Island Quilter's Guild to raise funds for the guild's educational programs, including scholarships for fine arts students at a local college. Coordinated by Marlene Haresign and Nancy McGann. Owned by Margaret Townsend. Photo by Morris Studio. Postcard available from Eastern Long Island Quilter's Guild, Box 1514, Southampton, NY 11968.

Color plate 15 *Sanibel Quilt*
Made by Sanibel Island, Florida, residents to raise funds to benefit the local library. Coordinated by Vera Graham, Shirley Evans, and Evelyn Klein. Photo by Mike Klein.

Appeared in *Quilter's Newsletter Magazine*, July/August 1981, and *Quilt* magazine, January 1982.

Color plate 16 *Marine Mammal Quilt*
Made to promote the work of the California Marine Mammal Society, Marin Headlands, Golden Gate National Recreation Area, Fort Cronkhite, CA 94965 by more than 60 marine mammal artists, appliqué specialists, and quilters. Coordinated by Peigin Barrett, the society's executive director. Photo by Susan Middleton. Posters, notecards, and holiday cards available from Lynn Dunn, Aquatique, 132 Clement St., San Francisco, CA 94118.

Color plate 17 *Caroline Lily*
A raffle quilt coordinated by a committee of five members of the Brooktondale Quilters, Community Center, Brooktondale, New York. Photo by Pat Valerio.

Color plate 18 *Mono Lake Quilt*
Made by quilters from the Golden Gate Audubon Conservation Committee and the East Bay Heritage Quilters. Designed by Ric Hugo and coordinated by Helen Green. Owned by Karen Rogers. Photo by Thomas Spillane.

Color plate 19 *Chaplin Elementary School Quilt*
Raffle quilt made by the Chaplin Quilters to benefit their town's elementary school. Designed by the children at the Chaplin Elementary School, Chaplin, Connecticut. Coordinated by Cathy Smith. Photo by Char Meyer.

Color plate 20 and figures 29 and 133 *Teachers' Centers Quilt*
Made by over 200 friends and colleagues of Kathleen Devaney upon the closing of the Teachers' Centers Exchange, which she had directed. Coordinated by Gretchen Thomas. Owned by Kathleen Devaney. Photos by Judy Robbins. Figure 29: Logo block from the New Haven, Connecticut, Teacher Center. Logo designed by Jan Murray and block made by Mary Eisenberg. Figure 133: Logo of the Teachers' Centers Exchange, block made by Gretchen Thomas.

Color plate 21 and figure 89 *Daisy Chain*
Patterns and quilt designed by Judy Martin. Quilt sewn by Mrs. R. M. Brown. Photos by Jerry De Felice. Appeared on the cover of *Quilter's Newsletter Magazine* April 1983, and in *Quiltmaker*, spring/summer 1982.

Color plate 22 *Origins*
Made by quilters of Humbolt County, California. Coordinated by Mary Ann Spencer. Photo by Lindsay Olsen.

Color plate 23 *Footlights at Wolf Trap*
Made by Quilters Unlimited as a fundraiser for Wolftrap Farm Park for the Performing Arts. Designed by Judy Spahn. Coordinated by Judy Spahn, Kay Walker. Annette Spitzer, and Nancy Nelson. Photo by Judy Spahn. Copyrighted 1983 by Judy Spahn.

Color plate 24 *Pueblo Indian Designs*
Made by 16 students in an Albany, California, adult ed-

ucation quilting class. Coordinated by Roberta Horton. Owned by Susan Arnold. Photo by Tony Henning.

Figure 1 *Green Acres Bird Quilt*
A baby quilt made by eight teachers at Green Acres Elementary School in North Haven, Connecticut, for Joseph, Ann, and Peter Diamantini. Coordinated by Shari Millen. Photo by Judy Robbins.

Figures 2, 36, and 37 *Dayton Historical Houses*
Made by members of the Dayton Historical Depot Society, a nonprofit corporation formed by local citizens to acquire and restore the oldest extant railroad station in the state of Washington. Coordinated and designed by Darlene Broughton and Faye Rainwater. Figure 2 photo by Professional Photography, Walla Walla, Washington. Figure 36: Peabody Hill block made by Lois Howard. Figure 37: First Baptist Church block made by Lena Hunt. Photos 36 and 37 by Darlene Broughton.

Figures 3 and 131 *Boone Bicentennial Sampler*
A 1976 bicentennial quilt for Boone County, Indiana. Designed by township committees and coordinated by Treva Iddings. Made by over 2,500 citizens of Boone County. Photos by Bass Photo, Indianapolis, Indiana. Detailed pamphlet with photos available from Treva Iddings, Box 366, Lebanon, IN 46052.

Figure 4 *Oberlin Quilt*
Designed and made by the Oberlin Quilters, Oberlin, Ohio. Coordinated by Ricky Clark. Photo by Jean Jones Tufts. Postcard available from The Oberlin Quilt, 291 Morgan St., Oberlin, OH 44074. Appeared in *Quilter's Newsletter Magazine*, 1974, *Ohio Quilts and Quilters 1980–1981*, *Ohio Quilts: A Living Tradition*, 1981, the *Oberlin Alumni Magazine*, September/October 1974, and *Pictorial Quilting* by Nina Holland, NY: A. S. Barnes, 1978.

Figure 5 Quilting the Hancock Quilt, which was made by the women of Hancock to celebrate the bicentennial of Hancock, New Hampshire. Artists' sketches by Grace Godwin Way and Dorothy Starratt. Coordinated by Lois Daloz and Betty Wells. Photo by John Stitch. Pictured left to right: Frances Russ, Lois Daloz, and Olive Rhines. Informational notecard available from the Hancock Historical Society, Hancock, NH 03449.

Figures 6 and 7 *Scenes of San Francisco*
Made as a raffle quilt to promote a quilt show by the San Francisco Quilters' Guild. Coordinated by Darlene Hartman. Owned by Miriam Weber. Figure 7: Golden Gate Bridge block by Lyn Piercy. Photos by Lynn Kellner and Susan Risedorph.

Figure 8 *Children's Stories*
Made by parents and teachers to raise funds for Washington Elementary School, Point Richmond, California. Coordinated by Rosemary Corbin. Photo by John Strayer.

Figure 9 *Rainbow Fantasy*
Yearly raffle quilt made by 17 parents of Thousand Oaks Elementary School PTA, Berkeley, California, to raise curriculum-enrichment funds. Design inspired by a rainbow quilt featured in *Quilter's Newsletter Magazine* and created by a committee of four. Coordinated by Kathy Tuttle. Central panel by Jan Inouye. Photo by Jan Inouye. Appeared in *Quilter's Newsletter Magazine*, October 1981.

Figure 10 *Flying Machines—Up, Up, and Away*
Yearly raffle quilt made by 16 parents of Thousand Oaks Elementary School PTA, Berkeley, California, for school curriculum-enrichment funds. Designed by a committee of five. Coordinated by Lynn Crook, Patty Gildersleeve, and Kathy Tuttle. Photo by Jan Inouye.

Figure 11 *Hat City Quilt*
Made by the Hat City Quilters, Danbury, Connecticut, to promote the activities of their guild. Designed and coordinated by Jackie Shailor. Photo by Judy Robbins.

Figure 12 *Bowers Museum Quilt*
Made to promote the Bowers Museum Shop, Santa Ana, California. Coordinated by Nancy Fister and Sally Arcolio. Photo by Stuart Weiner.

Figure 13 *Weathervane Quilt*
Made by The Quilter's Connection, Arlington, Massachusetts. Coordinated by Rachael Baumgartner and Pat Keane. Photo by Judy Robbins.

Figure 14 Summer Hill Quilters making the Bill O'Donnell Memorial Quilt to initiate and raise funds for the Bill O'Donnell Memorial Fund to benefit the Johns Hopkins Oncology Center. Pictured left to right: Pat O'Donnell and Dottie Hopkins. Photo by John Vennes.

Figure 15 A Brooktondale Quilters (Brooktondale, New York) quilting bee. Pictured: Eleanor Abbott, Margaret Adams, Sheilah Calza, Peggie A. Dunlop, Beverly A. Green, Louise Sharon Hoos, Deborah H. Stark. Photo by Bill Abbott.

Figure 16 *Mariner's Compass Quilt*
Made to raise funds for the Congregational Church in Portland, Connecticut, by the Congregational Church Women. Designed by Carolyn Johnson with help from Joy Rutty. Coordinated by Carolyn Johnson. Owned by Joy Rutty. Photo by Judy Robbins.

Figure 17 *No More Hiroshimas Peace Quilt*
Presented to the Hibakusha Support Home, Hiroshima, Japan, as a friendship gift from American quilters on the anniversary of the bombing of Hiroshima. Coordinated by Heidi Read, Diane Jones, and Anne Hausrath. Photo by Steven Welsh. Postcards of this and other peace quilts and Peace Quilters' Newsletter are available from the Boise Peace Project, 1820 N. 7th St., Boise, ID 83702.

Figure 18 *Texture of Fabric—Texture of Life; detail of central panel*
Designed and made by participants in the L.A. Theatre Works' Textile Arts Workshop at California Institution for Women, Frontera, California. Coordinated by artists Susan Hill and Terry Blecher, assisted by L.A. Hassing. Photo by Judith Pacht. The piece is available for exhibition. Statements from the participants accompany the work. For information on workshops and how to borrow the piece, contact L. A. Theatre Works, 681 Venice Blvd., Venice, CA 90291.

Figure 19 *Kathy Lord Campaign Quilt*
Made by supporters of the Kathy Lord for School Board campaign. Coordinated by Rosemary Corbin. Photo by John Strayer.

Figure 20 *Religious Symbols Quilt*
Made and owned by the quilting group at the Methodist Church of Dunes, Grand Haven, Michigan. Coordinated and designed by Betty Boyink. Photo by Brent Boyink.

Figure 21 *The Sun Sets on Sunbonnet Sue*
Made and owned by Seamsters Union Local #500, Lawrence, Kansas. Coordinated by Laurie Metzinger Schwarm and Barbara Brackman. Blocks from left to right, beginning at top left: (1) Self-immolation—Cathy Dwigans; (2) Dr. LaFong's Cure for Cuteness—Bryan Anderson; (3) O.D.—Nadra Dangerfield; (4) Skylab Accident—Carol Gilham; (5) Sunbonnet Soup—Betty Kelley; (6) Strangled by a Sunflower—Patty Boyer; (7) Food for Worms—Nadra Dangerfield; (8) Sunbonnet Sioux—Bonnie Dill; (9) Three Mile Island—Georgann Eglinski; (10) Eaten by a Snake—Nadra Dangerfield; (11) Mummified—Chickie Hood; (12) Struck by Lightning—Carol Gilham; (13) Tied to the Tracks—Georgann Eglinski; (14) Lost in Space—Bette Kelley; (15) Sunbonnet Sue-icide—Barbara Brackman; (16) Squashed by a Rock—Barbara Brackman; (17) Suestown, Guyana—Laurie Schwarm; (18) Jaws III—Nancy Metzinger; (19) Died for Love—Nadra Dangerfield; (20) Run-in with the Mob—Georgann Eglinski. Photo by Tim Forade. Postcards available from Prairie Flower Publishing, 500 Louisiana St., Lawrence, KS 66044. Appeared in *Quilter's Newsletter Magazine*, January 1983. Copyrighted 1979 by Seamsters Union Local #500, Lawrence, Kansas.

Figure 22 *Self-Portraits Quilt*
Designed and made by students in a K-1-2 class taught by Carol Smith Trimble at Peralta Year-round School, Oakland, California. Coordinated by Carol Smith Trimble. Photo by Judy Robbins.

Figure 23 *High Interest Rate*
A class project made by a 4-5-6 class taught by Mrs. Masuda at Franklin School, Berkeley, California, as part of a history unit. Coordinated by Jan Inouye. Photo by Jan Inouye.

Figure 24 Quilts made by Jean Linden and students at P.S. 48, Queens, New York. Pictured left to right: Jean Linden and Debbie McWilliams. Photo by Alyce Jackson, taken at the Washington, D.C., Department of Education.

Figure 25 *Ben Franklin Quilt*
Made by students at P.S. 48, Queens, New York, as a bicentennial quilt. Coordinated by Jean Linden. Photo by Judy Robbins.

Figure 27 *Nanny's Album Quilt*
Made by family members for Mary Duff. Designed and coordinated by Barbara Wysocki. Photo by Judy Robbins.

Figures 28, 33, 34 and 134 *Doris Kampe Friendship Quilt*
Made by the Granville Quilters for Doris Kampe, who now owns the quilt. Coordinated by Cindy Tavernise. Figure 33: Ball Jar block made by Verna Sadowski. Figure 34: Raspberries block made by Rosy Bacon. Figure 134: Sundial presentation block made by the Granville Quilters, Granville, Massachusetts. Photos by Judy Robbins.

Figure 29 (see color plate 20)

Figures 30, 31, and 135 *Bunce Family Anniversary Quilt*
Made by the Bunce family to celebrate their parents' 35th wedding anniversary. Coordinated by Mary Jo Deysach. Figure 30: Jim Payne's block. Figure 31: Sarah's block. Figure 135: Label block by Mary Jo Deysach. Photos by Mary Jo Deysach.

Figures 32 and 132 *Herb Society Quilt*
Quilt made by members of the Herb Society of America. Quilted by Carolyn Johnson. Coordinated by Betty Stevens. Figure 32: Onion block (logo of the Northern Illinois Herb Society unit), made by Joanna Reed. "Chicago" is a Native American word meaning "onion." Figure 132: Herb Society seal and logo block made by Hilda Wilson. Photos by Judy Robbins.

Figures 33 and 34 (see figure 28)

Figure 35 (see color plate 11)

Figures 36 and 37 (see figure 2)

Figures 38 and 39 (see color plate 2)

Figures 41, 42, 43, 44, and 45 *Five Variations: Star of the Sea*
Designed and made by Leslie C. Carabas. Quilted by Amanda Miller. In the collection of Mr. and Mrs. D. L. Commons. Photos by Leslie Carabas. Appeared in *Quilts: A Tradition of Variations*, a publication of the East Bay Heritage Quilters, 1982.

Figure 46 *Barely Enough*
Raffle quilt to raise funds for the East Bay Heritage Quilters. Made by guild members. Designed and coordinated by Jan Inouye and Ann Rhode. Photo by Jan Inouye.

Appeared in *Quilts: A Tradition of Variations,* a publication of the East Bay Heritage Quilters, 1982.

Figure 49 (see color plate 11)

Figure 50 *Claremont Quilt*
Made by mothers and friends of the Claremont (California) Stars Soccer Club to raise funds to send the team to Great Britain. Coordinated by Val Cressy and Sycha Spengemann. Photo by Wayne Book Photography.

Figure 79 *Snail Trail*
Made as a raffle quilt by members of the Unitarian-Universalist Society: East; Manchester, Connecticut. Co-ordinated by Judy Robbins. Owned by Carol Lacoss. Photo by Judy Robbins.

Figure 89 (see color plate 21)

Figure 97 *Friendship Quilt*
Owned by Ethel Stevens of Simsbury, Connecticut. Photo by Judy Robbins.

Figure 104 (see color plate 12)

Figure 110 *Ohio Star*
Raffle quilt made by 15 mothers and teachers at Keeney Street Elementary School, Manchester, Connecticut. Coordinated by Pat McNally and Wendy Palermo. Photo by Judy Robbins.

Figure 118 *Propeller*
Raffle quilt made by the Glastonbury Piecemakers, Glastonbury, Connecticut. Reproduced with permission of the owner, Crystal Bogosian. Photo by Judy Robbins.

Figure 130 *Our Valley; title and signature block*
Quilt made by 11 members of the Fresno Fiber Guild. Coordinated by Roxanne Barkofsky and Shirley Schramm. Title and signature block by Roxanne Barkofsky. Photo by Jane Erica Cody.

Figure 131 (see figure 3)

Figure 132 (see figure 32)

Figure 133 (see color plate 20)

Figure 134 (see figure 28)

Figure 135 (see figure 30)

Figure 136 (see color plate 11)

Resources for Group Quilters

Following are books, organizations, and other resources that will be of particular interest to cooperative quilters. Books mentioned in the text are listed here by author.

BOOKS AND HANDBOOKS

Avery, Virginia. *The Big Book of Appliqué.* New York: Charles Scribner's Sons, 1978.

Bank, Mirra. *Anonymous Was a Woman.* New York: St. Martin's Press, 1979.

Cohen, Cindy, ed., with woodcuts by Bonnie Acker. *From Hearing My Mother Talk: Stories of Cambridge Women.* The Cambridge Arts Council Fund, 1979. Cambridge Women's Commission, 57 Inman St., Cambridge, MA 02139.

Cooper, Patricia, and Norma Bradley Buferd. *The Quilters; Women and Domestic Art—An Oral History.* Garden City, NY: Doubleday, 1977.

Fanning, Robbie, and Tony Fanning. *The Complete Book of Machine Quilting.* Radnor, PA: Chilton Book Co., 1980.

Gobes, Sarah Doolan; Mickey Lawler; Sheila Meyer; and Judy Robbins. *Not Just Another Quilt.* New York: Van Nostrand Reinhold, 1982.

Holland, Nina. *Pictorial Quilting.* Cranbury, NJ: A.S. Barnes and Co., 1978. (Out of print. Available from interlibrary loan services.)

James, Michael. *The Quiltmaker's Handbook* and *The Second Quiltmaker's Handbook.* Englewood Cliffs, NJ: Prentice-Hall, 1978 and 1981.

Laury, Jean Ray. *Quilts and Coverlets.* New York: Van Nostrand Reinhold, 1970.

Leman, Bonnie. *Quick and Easy Quilting.* Wheatridge, CO: Moon Over Mountain, 1979.

Leman, Bonnie, and Judy Martin. *Taking the Math out of Making Patchwork Quilts.* Wheatridge, CO: Moon Over Mountain, 1981.

Leone, Diana. *The Sampler Quilt Book.* 1980. Leone Publications: 2721 Lyle Ct., Santa Clara, CA 95051, 1980.

Penders, Mary Coyne. *Quilts in the Classroom: A Guide to Successful Teaching.* Quiltwork Publications: 2600 Oak Valley Drive, Vienna, VA 22180, 1983.

Spencer, Mary Ann, and Mary Root Hall. *Group Quilt Handbook.* 1983. 3575 Harrison Avenue, Eureka, CA 95501. A 16-page handbook with timetable to assist in coordinating a group quilt project. Includes advice and examples of fundraising.

Sunset Books and *Sunset Magazine* editors. *Quilting: Patchwork and Appliqué.* Menlo Park, CA: Lane Publishing Co., 1982.

MAGAZINES, ARTICLES, AND FILMS

Lady's Circle Patchwork Quilts. A magazine published quarterly by Lopez Publications, Inc., 23 West 26th St., New York, NY 10010; Carter Houck, editor.

Leman, Bonnie. "Scorecard and Criteria to Use When Judging Quilts in Competition." *Quilter's Newsletter Magazine*, July–August 1983, p. 22. (Photocopies available from QNM, Box 394, Wheatridge, CO 80033.)

Quilt (magazine). Harris Publications, Inc., 79 Madison Ave., New York, NY 10016, Aloyse Yorko, editor.

Quilter's Newsletter Magazine. Leman Publications, Inc., Box 394, Wheatridge, CO 80033.

Quiltmaker. A pattern magazine, published quarterly by Leman Publications, Inc.; Box 394, Wheatridge, CO 80033

Quilts in Women's Lives. 16mm color film. 1980. Distributor: New Day Films, Box 315, Franklin Lakes, NJ 07417.

QUILT DESIGNS, HISTORIES, AND PATTERNS

Clauser, Janie, Treva Joan Iddings, Nancy Morton, and Larry Worcester, eds. *Boone Bicentennial Sampler.* 1976. Box 366, Lebanon, IN 46052.

Clyne, Patricia Edwards. *The Chester Historic Quilt.* 1982. Friends of the Chester Library, 49 Main St., Chester, NY 10918.

Cohen, Cindy, ed. *A Patchwork of Our Lives: Women's Stories in Words and Fabric,* and *The Cambridge Women's Quilt Project Catalogue.* Cambridge Women's Commission, 57 Inman St., Cambridge, MA 02139.

Miles, Elaine. *Many Hands: Making a Communal Quilt.* 1982, R & E Miles, Box 1916, San Pedro, CA 90733. 37 pages plus patterns, describing how twelve friends make a baby quilt.

Quilters of the Hudson Highlands. *A Rose Is a Rose Is a Rose Quilt.* Box 2711, Newburgh, NY 12550. Twenty rose appliqué patterns for a quilt-as-you-go cooperative quilt.

Santa Clara Valley Quilt Association. *I'd Rather Be Quilting, Books I–IV.* Members' original quilt designs. SCVQA, Box 792, Campbell, CA 95009.

Taft, Connie, ed., and Mary Helen Foster, project coordinator. *The Onondaga County, New York, Bicentennial Quilt.* Onandaga County Bicentennial Office, 6075 Pine Grove Rd., Clay, NY 13041.

Wiechec, Philomena. *Celtic Quilt Designs.* 1980. Celtic Designs Co., 19170 Portos Dr., Saratoga, CA 95070.

ORGANIZATIONS, MUSEUMS, AND ON-GOING PROJECTS THAT SUPPORT GROUP QUILTMAKING

The American Museum of Quilts and Related Arts. 225 El Paseo de Saratoga, San Jose, CA 95130. Founded in 1977 and operated by volunteers from the Santa Clara Valley Quilt Association.

Boise Peace Project and Peace Award Quilts. 1820 N. 7th St., Boise, ID 83702. Publishes newsletter linking peace quilt projects.

Common Threads: Oral History Workshops for all kinds of community groups, including quilters. The Cambridge, Massachusetts, Social History Resource Center. Cambridge Women's Commission, 57 Inman St., Cambridge, MA 02139.

Ronald McDonald Houses, coordinator, Bud Jones. 500 N. Michigan Ave., Chicago, IL 60611.

Teel, Odette. Coordinator of a research project on American group quilts made since 1950. Odette is collecting basic descriptive information and examples of different types of group work, as well as stories about the quiltmakers themselves. American Group Quilts, 6511 Driscoll St., Long Beach, CA 90815.

Through the Flower Corporation, Box 842, Benecia, CA 94510. Circulators of *The Honor Quilt*, which grew out of Judy Chicago's *Dinner Party*.

Metric Conversions

LINEAR MEASURE

1 inch = 1,000 millimeters = 2.54 centimeters
12 inches = 1 foot = 0.3048 meter
3 feet = 1 yard = 0.9144 meter

SQUARE MEASURE

1 square inch = 6.452 square centimeters
144 square inches = 1 square foot = 929.03 square centimeters
9 square feet = 1 square yard = 0.8361 square meter

Index